# A Place
# to Belong

# A Place to Belong

## REFLECTIONS FROM MODERN LATTER-DAY SAINT WOMEN

Edited by
Hollie Rhees Fluhman
Camille Fronk Olson

DESERET
BOOK

Deseret Book Company
Salt Lake City, Utah

# TO MY MUSES

Savannah, Grace, and Sadie Fluhman
who teach me what women can do

—HRF

# TO MY PARENTS

Roberta and Wayne Fronk
who taught me I could do anything

—CFO

Library of Congress Cataloging-in-Publication Data

Names: Olson, Camille Fronk, editor. | Fluhman, Hollie Rhees, editor.

Title: A place to belong : reflections from modern Latter-day Saint women / edited by Camille Fronk Olson, Hollie Rhees Fluhman.

Description: Salt Lake City, Utah : Deseret Book, [2019] | Includes bibliographical references. | Summary: "An anthology of experiences from modern women in The Church of Jesus Christ of Latter-day Saints"— Provided by publisher.

Identifiers: LCCN 2019033418 | ISBN 9781629726250 (trade paperback)

Subjects: LCSH: Mormon women—Religious life. | Women in the Mormon Church. | LCGFT: Essays.

Classification: LCC BX8643.W66 P53 2019 | DDC 289.3092/52 [B]—dc23

LC record available at https://lccn.loc.gov/2019033418

Printed in the United States of America
LSC Communications, Crawfordsville, IN

10   9   8   7   6   5   4   3   2   1

# CONTENTS

# INTRODUCTION

Everyone has a story. This book is a collection of stories of inspiration from women of different backgrounds illustrating how they navigate their twin commitments to faith and to women's issues. This project springs from a deep love and respect for The Church of Jesus Christ of Latter-day Saints and for the young women who constitute fifty percent of its future.

For some who struggle, faith and a commitment to women's issues appear incompatible. These essays illustrate the complementarity of the two. Most of us have family members or friends who straddle faith in the restored gospel and a modern world that seems incongruous. Many choose to stay and seek resolution, but sadly, too many leave. This volume of distinctive stories from women of faith provides evidence that there is not just one way to be a covenanted Latter-day Saint woman.

These diverse stories, written by women who inhabit a world lacking easy answers, illustrate to young women the multiple reasons to see that their place is *in* the Church regardless of their differences, questions, or struggles. The hope is for all young women to see that it is possible to be a thoughtful, confident, and intelligent woman who honors her faith in the gospel of Jesus Christ without compromising her ideals as a modern woman or her covenants with the Lord. We trust that writing about our wrestles with these sometimes competing goals might aid the rising generation in their tasks and choices ahead. In many ways, theirs is the next iteration of a defining struggle for Latter-day Saints: to balance loyalty to the Church and challenges facing all women.

In his address "A Plea to My Sisters," President Russell M. Nelson said: "My dear sisters, whatever your calling, whatever your circumstances, we need your impressions, your insights, and your inspiration. We need you to speak up and speak out in ward and stake councils. We need each married sister to speak as 'a *contributing* and *full* partner' as you unite with your husband in governing your family. Married or single, you sisters possess distinctive capabilities and special intuition you have received as gifts from God. We brethren cannot duplicate your unique influence."

As a preface to that plea, he quoted President Spencer W. Kimball from a sermon given in 1979: "Much of the major growth that is coming to the Church in the last days will come because many of the good women of the world . . . will be drawn to the Church in large numbers. This will happen to the degree that the women of the Church reflect righteousness and articulateness in their lives and to the degree that the women of the Church are seen as distinct and different—in happy ways—from the women of the world."

His concluding statement sums up the integral and critical influence of women in the Church: "My dear sisters, you who are our vital associates during this winding-up scene, the day that President Kimball foresaw is today. You are the women he foresaw! Your virtue, light, love, knowledge, courage, character, faith, and righteous lives will draw good women of the world, along with their families, to the Church in unprecedented numbers!"[1]

President Nelson clearly supports strong women who can build the kingdom. Women can find support in the desire for a voice and an amelioration of the inequalities we have faced through centuries of cultural and social injustices. In this volume, when the word *feminism* is used, it simply refers to a commitment to resolving the diverse issues facing women. The feminism that we speak of is neither critical nor hostile toward the leaders of the Church nor does it pigeonhole women into any one mold. The authors in this book echo the belief of acclaimed Latter-day Saint scholar Laurel Thatcher Ulrich that the principles of feminism are "compatible not only with the gospel of Jesus Christ but with the mission of The Church of Jesus Christ of Latter-day Saints."[2] Or, as Neylan McBaine, author of *Women at Church*, put it: "If you care about the spiritual, emotional and intellectual development opportunities available to you, your wife, your sister or your daughter, you are a feminist. Period. Based on this definition, the doctrine of The Church of Jesus Christ of Latter-day Saints is inherently feminist. The Lord cares about women, our leaders care about women and we as a people care about women."[3]

Whether a stay-at-home mom or a career woman, single or married, from Salt Lake City or Rome, the women in this volume share how they live their faith through everyday challenges that are uniquely theirs. Their stories show that we can all find identity and dignity in preserving our testimony of the Restoration as well as informing, adapting, and reconstructing our understanding of the gospel to meet the challenges of today.

Intellect and faith are not mutually exclusive but rather work together to create something stronger and more beautiful than either of them alone. For us, being committed members of The Church of Jesus Christ of Latter-day Saints is as much our identity as being a woman. There are choices to make in every aspect and stage of our lives. Nevertheless, we need not apologize for our faith traditions. Rather, there is power in identifying as both Latter-day Saint and woman.

Ours is a complex history. Many of our female predecessors dedicated their lives to the cause of women in the Church. Why then do so many women in the Church today feel marginalized? The Women's History division of the Church History Department recently produced several valuable historical resources about women. However, there is still a general ignorance regarding women's place in the Church, both historically and presently.

One of our most celebrated predecessors, Eliza R. Snow, instructed the Relief Society, "If any of the daughters and mothers in Israel are feeling in the least circumscribed in their present spheres, they will now find ample scope [as members of the Relief Society] for every power and capability for doing good with which they are most liberally endowed."[4]

Snow also encouraged her sisters, "Although we are not at present living up to all our privileges, and fulfilling all the duties that belong to our sex, the field is open before us, and we are urged to move forward as fast as we can develop and apply our own capabilities." These calls to action empowered women by encouraging them to take responsibility for change in their respective spheres. Snow located agency in the sisters themselves: "The difficulty is in getting the sisters to feel like undertaking it."[5] She sensed women of the Church possessed power to create positive change but worried that they would be their own stumbling block. Our hope is that the stories within this volume will remove that stumbling block.

A contemporary of Snow's, Emmeline B. Wells, called for gender equality when she wrote, "Let [woman] have the same opportunities for an education, observation and experience in public and private for a succession of years, and then see if she is not equally endowed with man and prepared to bear her part on all general questions socially, politically, industrially and educationally as well as spiritually."[6]

From her research on Wells, Carol Cornwall Madsen observed, "It was from the solidarity she felt within *both* her female and her Mormon cultures, not as a betrayal of either, that she expressed a strong feminist consciousness, fitting each within the scope of her own world view."[7]

Empowered by our similarities to these and many other women of our past, the women who tell their stories in this volume seek that same solidarity—to hear and be heard in a way that respects our foundational beliefs. Sharing stories is a poignant means of connection between women and our faith. We find commonalities and celebrate differences and, by giving them voice, reclaim the sacred space of our sisterhood. In that space, each woman's authentic story is honored, embraced, and put forward as a testament that individuality is an essential part of the faith journey.

Stories matter. These stories show the diverse and fluid paths women take as they practice their faith in a way that is authentic and grounded in the gospel of Jesus Christ but also in a way that may not fit a stereotypical mold. Somewhat paradoxically, individuality often offers points of connection with other women. In unexpected ways, what we thought was ours alone turns out to be the thing that resonates with our sisters. Ultimately, our differences in the Church may just draw us closer together in bonds of connection and belonging.

By discovering new ways to relate and belong, none of us will walk alone. When unattainable stereotypes are replaced with flesh-and-blood lives of complexity, struggle, and faith, the potential for real connection and for confidence in our individuality is multiplied. We hope that you, our reader, will be empowered to raise your own voice and forge your own path that leads you and others to Christ as you reimagine what it is to be a woman of faith.

## NOTES

1. Russell M. Nelson, "A Plea to My Sisters," *Ensign,* November 2015.

2. As quoted in *Mormon Feminism: Essential Writings,* edited by Joanna Brooks, Rachel Hunt-Steenblik, and Hannah Wheelwright (New York: Oxford University Press, 2015), 3.

3. Neylan McBaine, "A Moderate Mormon's Manifesto," *Feminist Mormon Housewives,* October 1, 2013, http://www.feministmormonhousewives.org/2013/10/a-moderate-mormons-manifesto/.

4. Eliza R. Snow, "Latter-day Saint Ladies of Utah," as cited in Kate Holbrook and Rebecca Ryan Clark, "A Wider Sphere of Action," in *Women and Mormonism,* edited by Kate Holbrook and Matthew Bowman (Salt Lake City: University of Utah Press, 2016), 177.

5. Snow, in Holbrook and Clark, "Wider Sphere of Action," 177.

6. Emmeline B. Wells, "Action or Indifference," *Women's Exponent* 5, no. 7 (September 1, 1876): 54, as cited in Carol Cornwall Madsen, "Emmeline B. Wells: Romantic Rebel," in *Supporting Saints: Life Stories of Nineteenth-Century Mormons,* edited by Donald Q. Cannon and David J. Whittaker (Provo, UT: BYU Religious Studies Center, 1985), 319.

7. Carol Cornwall Madsen, "'Feme Covert': Journey of a Metaphor," *Journal of Mormon History* 17 (1991): 51–52; emphasis added.

# DOING TRUTH

Beautiful as you are, there is more
to you than meets the eye.
Now, what are you going to do about it?

—*Elaine A. Cannon*

# Ambiguity

## VIRGINIA PEARCE COWLEY

Virginia Pearce Cowley is the third child of President and Sister Gordon B. Hinckley. She and her late husband, James R. Pearce, are the parents of six children and have twenty-seven grandchildren and one great-grandchild. A published author and former marriage and family therapist, Virginia served as first counselor in the General Young Women Presidency and as a full-time Public Affairs missionary for the Church. She is married to Joseph F. Cowley Jr.

Because of various Church assignments and life experiences, I've spent considerable time listening to, talking to, and thinking about us, the women of The Church of Jesus Christ of Latter-day Saints. This is what I know: We're not here by accident. We each have "one wild and precious life" to live.[1] We don't know how long it will be, but we believe within that life we have a great deal of responsibility for what we choose to do.

It seems to me that men in the Church, as a whole, have a pretty clear outline for their lives. Even though there is tremendous room for differences, weighing options, and making personal decisions, there are some pretty solid guideposts on the male path: priesthood ordination in the twelfth year with specific duties; a mission responsibility somewhere around eighteen or nineteen; marriage somewhere in their twenties, along with an obligation to seek training or education that will prepare them to provide for a family; and so on. And most men have a great deal of individual control over meeting those expectations.

On the other hand—for us women—well . . . Maybe a good word to describe our life's path as women is *ambiguity*. Ambiguity suggests a lack of clarity and uncertainty, and so often that's the name of the game for us.

Let's start with Eve. We know little about her and yet a lot. She was

3

noble and full of faith. She had a mission to fulfill—one on which the whole human race depended. We have no record of her angst as she grappled with the ambiguity facing her, but how could she not have made her choice without weighing the immediate and long-term consequences for her—for Adam—and for her unborn posterity?

In a smaller sense, you and I grapple with ambiguity regularly. Trying to make decisions and finding our way along a life path that isn't always clearly charted—and some of those markers, such as marriage and childbearing, often seem to be out of our control. Additionally, we happen to live in a place and time when women have more opportunities and options available than at any other time in the history of the world. And so, the combination of duties, God-given desires, and new opportunities creates increasing uncertainty. President M. Russell Ballard taught: "I realize that women often deal with a kind of ambiguity not necessarily faced by men, as there is an endless array of choices as well as uncertainties in front of you. This can be particularly challenging today because the world offers women an increasing number of opportunities—many more than were available to women a generation ago."[2]

And so we repeatedly ask the question: "Am I doing what God wants me to do with my precious life?" I hear that from my daughters and my friends, and it's written all over the pages of my journals. I'm quite sure, dear reader, that it's a question you may be asking.

And every time we try to answer the question, because we are women, we weigh all sorts of competing loyalties and the effect our choices might have on others. We have the gift—and sometimes the curse—of being constantly tuned in to relationships. If I go back to school, accept this promotion, have another child, take on a demanding Church calling . . . how will that affect my family, my future relationships, the happiness of others . . . and my own walk toward holiness?

So how do we navigate this uncertain and ever-changing individual path and not only tolerate ambiguity but celebrate it? Well, I'll tell you what I think. In fact, I'll tell you three things I've been thinking about and that you may want to consider.

## REJOICE IN AMBIGUITY AND EXPECT REVELATION

Ambiguity is a cause for celebration because over and over it invites us to seek revelation from God. Yes, we look around us to see what others do in similar circumstances or at similar ages, but this is My Path, not someone else's. You and I get to go to Him for personal revelation. And so seeking and receiving revelation becomes a critical skill for every woman to develop. Only through personal revelation can the Lord reveal His desires for our path ahead. Sister Julie B. Beck said, "The ability to qualify for, receive, and act on personal revelation is the single most important skill that can be acquired in this life."[3] And Sister Patricia T. Holland said, "I believe that every one of us has a specific mission to fulfill on this earth."[4] If we believe that we are sent here with a specific mission and assignments, we have to believe that He will reveal them to us piece by piece. In the words of one of my favorite hymns, "I do not ask to see the distant scene—one step enough for me."[5]

One of the great bonuses of receiving revelation by which we make life choices is that we are far less likely to look at the lives of others and envy them—or worse still, look at the lives of others and criticize their life choices. Sister Ruth Renlund taught, "There's no one way to be an LDS woman. Each has a right to personal revelation and is expected to use that. It should be personal, and we shouldn't let other people's comments shake our direction. I think women are particularly susceptible to that."[6] In a life path filled with ambiguity, in our insecurity about our own choices, we too often watch others with a measuring eye.

## REVIEW THE CERTAINTIES

In times of uncertainty, it's helpful for me to review the certainties. I particularly need to be reminded of the things I know for sure when I'm swimming in uncertain territory. I don't know what's on your list, but mine includes these certainties:

God is my Father, and He will stand by me. "When I cry unto thee, then shall mine enemies turn back: this I know; for *God is for me*" (Psalm 56:9; emphasis added). His Son Jesus Christ is my Redeemer. The Holy Ghost is my Comforter and Guide. The things I know for sure include my larger purpose on earth: To grow and learn and change to become more like God, to return to live in His presence, and to help others do the same.

And I am certain about the reality of personal revelation. I can never predict *how* He will speak to me, but I've lived long enough to be certain that He will. I also know that revelation flourishes in the soil of gospel living. President Russell M. Nelson gave us a glorious promise: "To be sure, there may be times when you feel as though the heavens are closed. But I promise that as you continue to be obedient, expressing gratitude for every blessing the Lord gives you, and as you patiently honor the Lord's timetable, you will be given the knowledge and understanding you seek. Every blessing the Lord has for you—even miracles—will follow. That is what personal revelation will do for you."[7]

Those are my bottom lines. They're not up for grabs. And when I speak them out loud, I feel a kind of settled peace that allows me to open my heart and with confidence—even excitement—embrace the ambiguities.

## SLOW DOWN—GRAPPLING WITH AMBIGUITY TAKES TIME AND ENERGY

At times the wrestle to find a path ahead comes because unexpected adversity simply stops us in our tracks. The future we had planned vanishes. I'm told that when animals are wounded, they "hug the ground" for a while. I don't know about you, but I've had that experience where something suddenly hits you in the stomach—something that catapults you into a new and frightening world and, for a bit, all you can do is hug the ground and wait. I think we can give ourselves permission to do that for whatever time it takes to gradually stop feeling numb. You will know how long . . . no one else does.

I clearly remember the weeks after my husband died as ground-hugging times. I remember wondering if I would ever be able to feel anything but heavy again . . . and then one day, walking down the street (I can tell you the exact place), the heaviness lifted. I felt light just long enough to know that it would come back to stay eventually—that I would feel an underlying joy and sense of well-being again. I like to think about the word *fallow*. A fallow field is one that is plowed and harrowed but left unsown for a time in order to restore its fertility.

You may not even need to hug the ground. Maybe you just need to slow down, if ambiguity comes because of adverse conditions. But even in the absence of difficulty, we each need to carve out regular quiet spaces and places in everyday life . . . to just think, to be still. I believe that's a prerequisite for hearing the voice of the Lord.

Elder M. Russell Ballard encouraged us: "If your life is void of quiet time, would you begin tonight to seek for some? . . . We all need time to ask ourselves questions or to have a regular personal interview with ourselves."[8] President Gordon B. Hinckley advised college students: "You need time to meditate and ponder, to think, to wonder at the great plan of happiness that the Lord has outlined for His children. . . . Our lives become extremely busy. We run from one thing to another. . . . We are entitled to spend some time with ourselves in introspection, in development. . . . Your needs and your tastes along these lines will vary with your age. But all of us need some of it."[9]

This isn't worry time. This isn't planning time. This is time to meditate, to open yourself to life and to Him.

Think about walking into nature when you're creating space and place for introspection. I know a therapist who advises her clients to walk outside and actually touch something in nature to quiet their anxiety. Rub a leaf in your hand. Feel grass under your feet. Turn your face to drink in the sun!

We *can* take joy in the ambiguity of our lives, reviewing the certainties and taking time regularly to simply let God in—to stop and contemplate Him and His majesty. To place our lives at His feet—in quiet spaces and places—in times of quiet reflection and meditation, free of the lists of endless tasks, claiming the privilege of personal revelation. And surely, in His own time, He will flood you and me with His life-giving spirit and nudge us forward, to lead each of us to fulfill our foreordained mission, to rejoice in our one wild and precious life!

NOTES

1. Mary Oliver, "The Summer Day," *New and Selected Poems, Volume One* (Boston: Beacon Press, 1992), 94.

2. M. Russell Ballard, "Women of Dedication, Faith, Determination, and Action," in *Between God and Us: How Covenants Connect Us to Heaven: Talks from the 2015 BYU Women's Conference* (Salt Lake City: Deseret Book, 2016), 138.

3. Julie B. Beck, "And upon the Handmaids in Those Days Will I Pour Out My Spirit," *Ensign*, May 2010.

4. Patricia T. Holland, "A Woman's Perspective on the Priesthood," *Ensign*, July 1980.

5. John Henry Newman, "Lead, Kindly Light," *Hymns* (Salt Lake City: The Church of Jesus Christ of Latter-day Saints, 1985), no. 97.

6. Ruth L. Renlund, "Just Call Me Ruth," *Mormon Women Project*, May 2010, https://mormo nwomen.com/interview/just-call-me-ruth/.

7. Russell M. Nelson, "Revelation for the Church, Revelation for Our Lives," *Ensign*, May 2018.

8. More of Elder Ballard's remarks in their context: "The people of earlier times experienced solitude in ways we cannot imagine in our crowded and busy world. Even when we are alone today, we can be tuned in with our handheld devices, laptops, and TVs to keep us entertained and occupied.

    "As an Apostle, I now ask you a question: Do you have any personal quiet time? I have wondered if those who lived in the past had more opportunity than we do now to see, feel, and experience the presence of the Spirit in their lives.

    "Seemingly, as our world gets brighter, louder, and busier, we have a greater challenge feeling the Spirit in our lives. If your life is void of quiet time, would you begin tonight to seek for some? . . . We all need time to ask ourselves questions or to have a regular personal interview with ourselves. We are often so busy and the world is so loud that it is difficult to hear the heavenly words 'be still, and know that I am God'" (M. Russell Ballard, "Be Still, and Know That I Am God" [Church Educational System devotional for young adults, May 4, 2014, broadcasts.churchofjesuschrist.org]).

9. Gordon B. Hinckley, "Life's Obligations," *Ensign*, February 1999.

# Coming Home

## LANAE VALENTINE

LaNae Valentine holds a doctoral degree in marriage and family therapy and specializes in working with women struggling with depression, anxiety, perfectionism, body image, and eating problems. She enjoys homemaking, cooking, gardening, reading, yoga, road cycling, traveling, and spending time with family and friends.

Life is more complicated for girls and young adult women today than it used to be. In many ways, it's better. They have more opportunities and encouragement to achieve them than ever before. Many of them are walking through open doors that were closed to previous generations. They are being told from a young age that they can do whatever they want. They can shatter glass ceilings, even become president of the United States! Parents and teachers encourage them to be confident, to speak up, and achieve great things. Girls are cheered on to "play any sport, join any after-school club, volunteer for any cause and to get good grades." Currently, "girls are regularly outperforming boys in school and enrolling in higher numbers in college." It's a great time to be a woman—or is it? "Because behind all these possibilities is a troubling development"—rising rates of anxiety, depression, and suicide.[1]

When I was growing up in the 1960s, Betty Friedan, an early feminist, articulated "the problem with no name" as the pressure women experienced to feel fulfilled only by their roles as wives and mothers. It seems that today, nearly fifty years later, we have a new problem with no name, the pressure to feel fulfilled by "having it all."

Millennials are growing up with oversized expectations of personal and professional success. "Twice as many girls as boys reported that they felt depressed frequently or occasionally, and twice as many girls as boys said they were overwhelmed with all they had to do." Millennials are feeling the most pressure, reporting that they feel "extreme" pressure to succeed. They report an overall mood of anxiety, feelings of self-reproach, and beliefs that they haven't done enough yet and time is running out.[2]

The pressure to be great at everything is causing many to feel less confident, more fearful of failure, and more critical of themselves. On the surface, they seem exceptional, but internally they are anxious and stressed—feeling that no matter how hard they try, they will never be smart enough, pretty enough, thin enough, or popular enough. If a girl is tuned in to popular culture, she is learning distorted ideas about what it takes to be a success.

Social media is just another platform where a girl or young woman is expected to perform, achieve, and compare herself to others. Social media rewards behaviors that girls have long been primed to express: pleasing others, seeking feedback, performing, and looking good. The very bones of the internet reflect and intensify the fruitless drive for perfection. Online, as in real life, there will always be someone thinner, more successful, in a better relationship, with more friends, and doing more fun things than you. Those who spend significant time on social media are more prone to withdraw from the essential relationships that offer solace and support.

In my experience, I have found certain behaviors beneficial to successfully navigating life and fostering relationships that offer real solace, support, and self-esteem. At the top of my list is establishing a relationship with God.

If we don't have a relationship with God, if we don't think He loves us, if we can't see our great potential, we'll turn from Him and seek love, worth, and validation in all the wrong places. When we can't hear God's answers or trust His promises, we block our relationship of grace and are left to do everything on our own. We may turn away when we feel the weight of our imperfections, when we keep messing up repeatedly, and when we feel less than we should be. We start to believe He must be displeased or even mad at us. At the core of our turning away is a misunderstanding of who God really is.

Often, our views of God are influenced by attitudes and practices of parents, caretakers, teachers, and other authority figures. Sometimes we weren't accurately taught about who God is. Like the Pharisees of Jesus's day, I was taught to see God as a scorekeeper who keeps tabs on all I do. I saw Him as absent, unavailable, and hard to reach. We can lose faith in Him because we fear He won't give us the beautiful life we desire. We fear His path to happiness will be less exciting and fulfilling and full of sacrifice and hardship.

Whatever the reason for turning from God, we can start now to foster a relationship with Him—even if we're not sure we believe in God, even if our relationship with Him is shaky or nonexistent, even if we're mad at Him or think He's mad at us, even if it bothers us that God is a Man and we worship Him as our Father while neglecting the existence of our Heavenly Mother. We can start by making time to quiet the mind and allow ourselves to feel. Shutting out our anxious thoughts requires practice.

I have found mindfulness to be helpful when prayer is difficult. Mindfulness is holding still, being present, and letting go of judgments, expectations, and anxious thoughts. Several apps and scripts for practicing mindfulness and meditation are available. Some scripts focus on gratitude, forgiveness, and appreciation for the body. They help me come into alignment with God and my inner spirit. "*Be still, and know that I am God*" (Psalm 46:10; emphasis added) is one of them. For me, this passage means to stop striving, let go, surrender, and trust in God to provide me with help, strength, and safety.

There is a deeper dimension to stillness than our external posture. In essence, it's a state of relaxation and surrender. We can relax our grip and trust we are in God's hands. Completely trusting Him can be a pretty hard thing to do. Or it can be the most exciting, thrilling thing we can ever do. As the scripture promises, "Thou shalt abide in me, and I in you" (Moses 6:34). God can live in us and work through us.

A book by C. Baxter Kruger called *The Parable of the Dancing God* helped me correct my understanding of God. The book's focus is on the parable of the prodigal son found in Luke 15. Kruger believes this story is not really about either the prodigal or the older son. Rather, he suggests that the parable's central figure is the father, as a type of our Heavenly Father. The story therefore illustrates the way God thinks and the way God acts toward us.

When the prodigal son returns to his father's home, hoping that his father will accept him even as a humble servant, the father's response is noted in the story. Kruger believes this response provides the greatest statement about God in the whole Bible: "But while he was still a long way off, his father saw him, and was moved with compassion for him, and ran and embraced him and kissed him" (Luke 15:20, New American Standard Bible, online).

What a picture of a loving father! He is absolutely thrilled to see his wayward son. He dishes out no reproaches or rebukes. He gives no test to prove the son is truly repentant. Instead, the father declares that this son be clothed in the best attire and the family ring placed on his finger. Then he proclaims a celebration because "my son was lost, but now is alive." Like the father in the parable, God is a joyful, loving Father who steadfastly, persistently, and unswervingly remains exactly what He is, a Father, even and especially when His sons and His daughters lose their way or rebel against Him.

Like the prodigal son, we may avoid God because we fear His response to us. We think He loves us or does not love us for what we do. We fear he stops loving us when we rebel or fail. But He is our Father—no matter what. He does not keep a scorecard on us in His heart. This realization was earth-shattering for me because I had been taught the legalistic religious steps to forgiveness. These steps seemed impossible to complete for the anxious, perfectionistic person I was. It didn't seem like I could ever do enough to be worthy and acceptable to God. When I lacked forgiveness, I assumed it was because I wasn't sorrowful enough, hadn't done enough to make restitution, hadn't wrestled or suffered like Enos or Alma the Younger. I no longer see repentance or forgiveness or God this way.

Heavenly Father promises, "I will also be your light in the wilderness; and I will prepare the way before you" (1 Nephi 17:13). I like to think of this inner guidance system that God has given us as an internal GPS system. When I travel back to my hometown in Colorado, I rely on the GPS on my phone to navigate some tricky twists and turns along the way. Invariably, I make a wrong turn. When that happens, a nice voice informs me that I'm off course and tells me how to get back on course. Rarely do I have to go all the way back to the place where I made the wrong turn. Never does the GPS rebuke me or make me feel I'm stupid, directionally challenged, or a horrible driver. So I never think, "I give up. I'll never make it to Colorado."

I have learned to rely on God's guidance, which comes as thoughts to my mind or as feelings or impressions to my heart, when I learn from commandments, general conference, and speakers and lessons at church. I have found that this inner guidance is always accompanied by feelings of peace. To keep me listening to this divine internal guidance, I strive to remember the picture of my compassionate, dancing, and joyful Father running to embrace and kiss and kiss and kiss me. Doing so changes everything.

## NOTES

1. Kelly Wallace, "Tackling the Relentless Pressure to Succeed That's Driving Girls to Despair," CNN, February 28, 2018, https://www.cnn.com/2018/02/28/health/girls-perfection-depression-anxiety/index.html.
2. Wallace, "Tackling the Relentless Pressure to Succeed."

# Prodigal Laundry

## LUISA PERKINS

Luisa Perkins is the author of *Prayers in Bath, Dispirited*, and the cookbook *Comfortably Yum*. She holds an MFA in writing from Vermont College of Fine Arts, Montpelier, Vermont. She teaches early morning seminary in Pasadena, California. Luisa and her husband, Patrick, are the parents of six children.

Tess Perkins

You asked me why I believe in miracles. The bottom line is laundry. Really. I'll tell you the story.

Picture me in my shadowed bedroom, on my knees, begging. "Help me. Please." Hoping God wouldn't mind my not having prettier words.

You know how it is with roommates. Sometimes it's impossible to swim against the current. I knew I had to make a change, but I didn't know how. Couldn't afford to move; could not afford to stay.

God was my last chance. I didn't think I deserved an answer. But I couldn't see my way out of that bad place on my own. "Help me," I repeated.

*Do your laundry,* came a voice. Clear. Calm. Ordinary.

Laundry. God's answer was laundry.

"Seriously?" I asked.

*Do your laundry.*

Fine. Okay. Whatever.

I stood up, stuffed my dirty clothes into a grocery bag, dug some quarters out of a jar, and went down to the little building in the middle of the palm-treed courtyard.

A thrumming dryer was my only company. I got my wash started, then looked more closely at that dryer. I recognized what was tumbling inside. A half-remembered seminary scripture came to mind. Garments washed white through the blood of the Lamb.

"I see where You're going with this," I whispered.

I sat down on a broken plastic chair and kept my eyes on that dryer as if it were a magic portal. Picture me breathing in bleach and mold, waiting.

A half hour later, a woman came in, opened the dryer, and pulled out a handful of clothes.

I cleared my throat and swallowed. "Hey." My voice came out ragged and crusty.

She turned around. Her gaze was open. No caution, no suspicion. "Hi," she said.

"You're Mormon," I said.

She side-eyed her laundry basket, more guarded now. "Yeah."

My story spilled out—my bad choices, my feeble hopes for making things right. Totally oversharing, past pride, past shame.

She listened, didn't shrink away. Her face shone with something I'd almost forgotten.

"So," I finished, "I wondered if you could tell me the name of your bishop? Maybe your ward has a housing specialist you could connect me with?"

She looked at me for a few seconds, which only seemed like a week. I was about to mumble "Never mind," when she smiled.

She introduced herself, hesitated, and then went on. "The girl who shared my apartment just got married and moved out. Today I was going to put up a flyer for a new roommate. Do you have a job?"

I nodded.

She told me how much the rent was. "Can you manage that?"

I nodded again. "That's how much I'm paying now."

She glanced at my washer, chugging away off balance. "While your laundry's going, you could come see the place. If you like it, the room's yours."

No references? No ID? No deposit? I couldn't believe she'd trust me like that.

"Wow," I said. "Okay."

She picked up her basket. "Come on."

We walked toward my wing of the apartment complex. She went in the main door. Up the stairs two flights to my floor, down my hall. Wait, really? I started to wonder whether this was some elaborate joke.

But at the door across from mine, she stopped and fished out keys. "Here it is."

Inside was my apartment's mirror image. She showed me a bedroom exactly like mine.

Not exactly. Picture me staring into a space empty of everything but light and promise.

"What do you think?"

"It's perfect," I whispered.

"Great." She beamed and stuck out her hand. "Welcome home."

Turning your life around can be a long journey, but sometimes God knows all you have the strength for is a load of laundry.

Do I still have questions, still wrestle with doubt? The bottom line is yes. But the thing I know for sure is this. When I asked, Someone answered with a miracle.

# DIVINE IDENTITY

It is the Spirit who reveals to us our identity—
which isn't just who we are but who we have
always been. And that when we know, our
lives take on a sense of purpose so stunning
that we can never be the same again.

—*Sheri L. Dew*

# My Identity as a Daughter of Heavenly Parents

## SAHAR QUMSIYEH

Jeff Smith

Sahar Qumsiyeh was born to Christian parents in Palestine and joined The Church of Jesus Christ of Latter-day Saints while pursuing a master's degree at Brigham Young University, Provo, Utah. She is the author of *Peace for a Palestinian: One Woman's Story of Faith amidst War in the Holy Land.* Sahar holds a PhD in statistics from the Middle East Technical University, Ankara, Turkey, and is a faculty member in the mathematics department at BYU–Idaho, Rexburg, Idaho.

I am a Palestinian Arab. Four years before I was born, my entire country was occupied by Israel. That meant that my country, Palestine, suddenly did not exist on a map. Our nationality was no longer valid, and our flag was banned. I felt like an outsider in my own country. I struggled to belong in the very place I call home. The happiness I felt when I saw my flag raised high did not last, because Israeli soldiers would often spot the flag and make us take it down—at gunpoint—and burn it. A piece of me died every time I saw my beloved Palestinian flag burned.

I was born in Jerusalem and grew up in a little town called Beit Sahour, close to Bethlehem. My town is where the shepherds watched their flocks when angels appeared to inform them about the birth of our Savior. At that time, angels sang, "Glory to God in the highest, and on earth peace, good will toward men" (Luke 2:14). The peace the angels sang about was something I never experienced. As I was growing up, my life was filled with demonstrations, tear gas, curfews, restrictions, and sounds of gunshots. I felt that God had abandoned me and my people. I often went on demonstrations to demand freedom and the right to fly my flag, to have an identity and a nationality. I desired that so much. I wanted to belong to a place that I could call home, a place where I could live with respect.

I was thrilled to receive a scholarship to study at Brigham Young University. I felt impressed to go to BYU, even though I was not a member of The Church of Jesus Christ of Latter-day Saints. My mother tried to convince me to turn down the offer because, she said, Utah was a desert and no one lives there. Despite some discouragement from family and friends, I listened to the feeling in my heart and went to BYU anyway. The first time I entered the United States, I was carrying various forms of identification. I had a Jordanian passport, but I was not Jordanian. I also had an Israeli travel document, but I was not Israeli. The immigration officer, likely confused, asked me, "Ma'am, what is your nationality?" I looked at him, unsure of what to answer. Saying "I am Palestinian" was not valid because my country did not exist anymore and my nationality was no longer recognized. I looked into his eyes with a questioning look on my face. The officer, thinking I didn't understand his English, repeated his question, now more slowly. "What— is—your—nationality?" I still looked at him, still confused, but finally uttered, "I'm Palestinian." Now it was his turn to be confused because he didn't seem to know what that meant. It took him a while before he finally said, "Oh, West Bank." His answer at least meant he knew where I came from.

I didn't know anything about The Church of Jesus Christ of Latter-day Saints when I arrived in Provo, Utah. I was worried about fitting into a strange culture among people of a different faith. People at BYU were really nice, but I still felt different. The girls in my dorm talked about dating, boys, shopping, and clothes. Those were things I considered to be of little importance. My country was under occupation, and my people were being shot and persecuted as they fought for their freedom. How could I think about anything else?

I had beliefs different from those of my fellow students at BYU, even though they were Christian like me. They talked to me about a loving God, one who answers prayers. I believed in God but never thought God would care about me, a Palestinian. I had often prayed to Him asking Him to end my life. I was so depressed in Palestine and simply wanted to end my misery. He never answered and never gave me any indication that He cared.

While in the United States, I went to Independence Day celebrations with my friends. As I looked at the parade and the American flags flying, I tried to imagine what it would be like if this were a celebration of my people's independence, of the creation of a Palestinian state. I tried to imagine how I would feel if the colors that were raised were not red, white, and blue but rather black, red, green, and white. As the fireworks sounded in my ear and their beautiful colors filled the air, I could not stop tears from rolling down my face because I realized I would never know what that felt like. I wanted to ask the Americans there to tell me what it is like to belong to a country, to be free, and to have a nationality. Instead I chose to watch them and imagine their feelings with tears in my eyes.

I watched the American children having fun and laughing at the parade and realized this happiness was something I had never seen in Palestinian children. Our children grow up in a place of conflict surrounded by walls and checkpoints, and their childhood is stripped from them. Even the beauty all around them has been taken. With the separation wall surrounding Bethlehem, there are very few fields or trees to be seen. While living in Palestine, I never saw a bird with color. All birds are brown. All butterflies are white. Even the very colors and beauty have been taken away from our lives.

While I was at BYU, my friends told me they were going to listen to general conference and said that their prophet was going to speak. Out of curiosity, I went with them to listen. When I heard an apostle in one conference talk refer to my country as Palestine, I was intrigued. President Gordon B. Hinckley said in that conference, "Jesus is the Christ, the promised Messiah, who came to earth in the most humble of circumstances, who walked the dusty roads of Palestine teaching and healing, who died upon Golgotha's cruel cross and was resurrected the third day."[1] Wanting to find out more, I asked my friend Shae about her faith. Shae taught me about the plan of salvation and about the loving God she believes in. She taught me that I am a daughter of Heavenly Parents, that They love me and want me to be happy. After investigating the Church for some time, I was baptized in February of 1996.

Knowing that I was a daughter of God made all the difference in my life. I had finally found the identity I had been seeking. I was a daughter of an All-Powerful King who loved me. It no longer mattered that I had neither nationality nor passport. I knew who I was and to whom I belonged. I belonged to the kingdom of God and had a just King who was merciful, loving, kind, and all-powerful—the Lord Jesus Christ. This was an identity that no occupation, no humiliation, no political dehumanization, and no injustice could take away from me.

"The Family: A Proclamation to the World" says, "All human beings—male and female—are created in the image of God. Each is a beloved spirit son or daughter of heavenly parents, and, as such, each has a divine nature and destiny."[2] That divine nature each of us has helps us rise above any trial and survive any storm we may face.

When I returned home to Palestine after joining the Church, my family tried everything in their power to convince me to leave the Church. They threatened to burn my scriptures and did not speak to me every weekend because I went to church. In addition to that, I felt isolated from other members of the Church because the only branch was at the BYU Jerusalem Center, about seven miles from my home. Because I am Palestinian, Israeli soldiers prevented me from entering Jerusalem. Every Sabbath I sneaked around checkpoints and across rocky fields to get to church. This involved a three-hour trip that also included climbing hills and walls while hiding from soldiers. Sometimes I was shot at and almost arrested. For twelve years I went through these trials, but I felt the loving arms of my Heavenly Father around me every day. I felt a strength that came from sources that only He can provide. Even when things were hard, I knew my Heavenly Parents loved me and that I was Their daughter. They were aware of what I was going through. God's mighty hand could have made my trials disappear and my mountains move from before me. Instead, because of His infinite love, He often chose to let me climb those mountains so I could grow and become more like Him. Elder Dieter F. Uchtdorf said: "Wherever you are, whatever your circumstances may be, you are not forgotten. No matter how dark your days may seem, no matter how insignificant you may feel, no matter how overshadowed you think you may be, your Heavenly Father has not forgotten you. In fact, He loves you with an infinite love. Just think of it: You are known and remembered by the most majestic, powerful, and glorious Being in the universe! You are loved by the King of infinite space and everlasting time!"[3]

I testify that we are sons and daughters of a Heavenly King. Our Heavenly Father is all-powerful, and He loves us. I testify that the Savior, the creator of this earth, was born in my little town of Bethlehem; that He suffered, died, and was laid in a tomb. That tomb is now empty; I have seen it. It is empty because our Savior broke the bands of death and rose triumphant from the grave. He suffered in Gethsemane for your sins and for mine. He felt your pains and each of your challenges. He knows you and He loves you. You are of royal lineage and have a divine nature within you. Nothing anyone does or says to you can ever change that.

## NOTES

1. Gordon B. Hinckley, "This Work Is Concerned with People," *Ensign*, May 1995.
2. "The Family: A Proclamation to the World," *Ensign*, November 2010.
3. Dieter F. Uchtdorf, "Forget Me Not," *Ensign*, November 2011.

# A Feminist

## KATE HOLBROOK

As a managing historian at the Church History Department of The Church of Jesus Christ of Latter-day Saints, in Salt City, Utah, Kate Holbrook studies the ways Latter-day Saint women make meaning and shape history. She has coedited several books, including *At the Pulpit: 185 Years of Discourses by Latter-day Saint Women*. Her principal research interests are religion, women, and food.

Recently one of my favorite editors at work asked me, reasonably, to do what felt impossible. He was responding to a piece I'd written about the 1960s and '70s, one in which I described Church leaders' grappling with the women's movement of that period. He noticed that I hadn't adequately defined what the cultural movement, often called Second Wave Feminism, stood for. I knew he was right, and I immediately plunged mentally into the emotional and intellectual context of an embarrassing moment from a decade earlier.

I had moved to Utah with my husband and was caring for our three very young children while writing my PhD dissertation on the radical food habits of Latter-day Saints and Black Muslims. Afterward, I returned to Boston, my home for a decade and the city of my graduate program, to deliver a speech on twentieth-century feminism. My friend Laurel Thatcher Ulrich was going to miss my talk, so I described the highlights to her. I summarized what I thought I knew about Second Wave Feminism, including that it had led proponents to devalue traditional women's contributions, such as childcare and the domestic arts. Laurel became suddenly still. A quality of hers that I would love to emulate is her ability to nurture while correcting an error. Over and again I have seen her clearly and graciously dismantle false understandings. That is what she did with me then, reminding me how many of her colleagues participated in the Second Wave Women's Movement by un-covering and celebrating centuries of female contribution, both private and public. Immediately I thought of her own body of work, so focused on the meanings and value of female occupations, for which she had been awarded the history field's most prestigious honors: the Pulitzer, the Bancroft, a MacArthur "genius" grant. In their effort to overturn the systematic devaluation of women, some feminists had denigrated "women's work," but certainly not all of them did. I felt embarrassed that the impromptu summary of my talk had been so limited and I so blind. The range of beliefs represented by the word *feminist* is part of what made defining that term so daunting. And so was the danger that I would again misstep and not do justice to the brave people who came before me.

Perhaps the hardest aspect of the task was deciding whether to de-fine the term in a way that included me. Even back in the twilight of my teen years, I understood well the short step from calling a woman "feminist" to demonizing her. I was initially wary of feminists myself. When a trusted friend encouraged me to take a class from a feminist professor at Brigham Young University, I agonized over what travesties might take place in that classroom. But I registered for the course and then for two others from the same professor. The study of literature un-der her tutelage taught me to be a grownup. As a child, I had absorbed a definition of the feminine that made a high priority of pleasing men. I deferred to men's opinions even when a voice inside me suspected they were wrong. But—and this made it a little easier—when they were wrong, I wasn't culpable because I had done the right thing in deferring to them. Feminism pulled me into a higher accountability, insisting that I had choices and was responsible for them. Feminism also gave me a sense of mission. I saw how women were vulnerable and had been short-changed. I wanted what was best for women, because I thought that was ultimately best for men and children as well.

Even the minor early fruits of this transition felt substantial. For the first time, on a date I asked whether I could turn down the heat in the car when it felt too warm. Most of the young men I went out with were grateful—they had turned up the heater out of consideration, to make me comfortable, and without my speaking up, they had nothing to go on. Speaking up led to meaningful conversation, compromise, and progress well beyond climate control in a car.

My new, feminist, increased understanding of personal accountability made me feel like a better Latter-day Saint. Agency was a core gospel teaching, and there were times that I had cheated it. Thinking through the conditions that most help women to realize their potential, I saw how my religious upbringing contributed to this process. We learned to study, to preach, and to teach from a very young age. Except when some flawed understanding of gender roles adulterated the doctrine for some of us, as it had for me, we assumed accountability at age eight. We were taught to avoid circumstances that would make us vulnerable to others' manipulations of our bodies through sex or addiction. In the Young Women program, we learned to imagine good lives for ourselves and figure out what steps to take to realize our aspirations. A whole community stood by to support us. Jesus stood closest of all to restore us when we inevitably failed. I hadn't dismissed agency before, but now I really embraced it. My salvation was up to me. My ability to do good in the world depended on me. My happiness, well, it was mine to choose. I felt and thought that these changes made Jesus happy. I called myself a feminist and felt divine approval for doing so.

Years later and still a feminist, I helped to plan and teach a popular religion course to which the professor and I invited a number of guest lecturers, giants in their respective fields, most of whom sacrificed personal comfort in pursuit of a better world. Katha Pollitt, a writer for *The Nation* magazine, confirmed for me that it was not just within my Utah Latter-day Saint culture that the word *feminist* invited listeners to demonize a person. Pollitt described to hundreds of students in that Harvard auditorium how few people were willing to call themselves feminist because of their false ideas about what a feminist was: a bra-burner, a man-hater, ugly. Pollitt said these stereotypes of feminists not caring about their appearance were misleading. "That stereotype is used to say to young women, 'If you call yourself a feminist, you are not going to have a boyfriend; you are not going to get married; you are not going to have children. You are just going to be lonely and miserable.'

That is not true at all."[1] Being afraid of the word would lead us to miss solutions still needing to be sought, she warned us. I celebrated her words because I felt they were important and, to be honest, because they made me feel good about myself. I called myself a feminist. I brought my infant daughter to class so that some of the magic there might rub off on her and so that students could see me happily combining parenting and teaching.

Nevertheless, I always saw how the label could be divisive. After joining the Church History Department at Church headquarters as a full-time employee, I wondered whether I should still call myself a feminist. How many people would close their eyes to my work because of their mistaken assumptions about feminism? And what about assumptions that weren't wrong? When Katha Pollitt came to Utah on a book tour, she expressed deep loyalty to a social policy that I thought was detrimental. There were feminists with whom I disagreed about women's issues. In the name of feminism, one person wrote a celebrated book that I found coarse and destructive. I saw young scholars invoke feminism to set courses that could only lead to a world full of lonely, suffering narcissists and those too poor and abandoned to become such. But there were also the feminist speakers and writers whose wisdom rang true and made my heart sing.

Would it jeopardize my Church affiliation to call myself feminist? The Church of Jesus Christ of Latter-day Saints facilitated my relationship with the divine and with other people better than any organization I knew personally or had studied academically. Step by step, my church participation made me closer to the person I longed ultimately to become. The Church was (is!) dear to me, precious, and filled my life with beauty. With the original Second Wave founders of *Exponent II*, I held my Church and my feminism as deeply compatible: "*Exponent II*, poised on the dual platforms of Mormonism and Feminism, has two aims: to strengthen The Church of Jesus Christ of Latter-day Saints, and to encourage and develop the talents of Mormon women. That these aims are consistent we intend to show by our pages and our lives."[2] Religious thinking motivated many early proponents of Second Wave feminism.[3] Religious values could help us to maintain community, forgiveness, and charity in our feminism.

If I declined to call myself a feminist, I would be turning my back on the efforts of my foremothers, those who shared my religious affiliation and those who did not. To reject the term felt like a lie, as if I were saying there was no more work to do on women's behalf. We humans have made progress but not yet achieved the temporal and spiritual redemption for women that Eliza R. Snow, Emmeline B. Wells, and others, including me, believe was set in motion when Joseph Smith proclaimed to the Nauvoo Relief Society, "I now turn the key to you in the name of God, and this Society shall rejoice, and knowledge and intelligence shall flow down from this time."[4]

Disowning the label risked participating in the easy demonization of women, defining their careful and heartfelt responses to difficult questions by what was inevitably left incomplete in their solutions. How can a neat solution to such difficult questions exist in the context of this fallen world we inhabit? Maybe such solutions do exist, but our diverse global society is not yet able to implement them whole. Trial and error, making us gradually better, does happen. My life's work has been to understand and write about the past so that we humans can more wisely build the future.

Today I define feminism as a dedication by women and men to pursue changes that will acknowledge the full humanity of women, promote women's educational and spiritual development as agents, and encourage women's full participation in society. I plant myself hopefully within this feminism's borders.

## NOTES

1. *Global Values 101: A Short Course*, edited by Ann Kim, Kate Holbrook, Brian Palmer, and Anna Portnoy (Boston: Beacon Press, 2006), 151, 158–59.
2. Claudia L. Bushman, "*Exponent II* Is Born," *Exponent II* 1, no. 1 (July 1974): 2.
3. Ann Braude, "Religions and Modern Feminism," in *Encyclopedia of Women and Religion in North America,* vol. 1, edited by Rosemary Skinner Keller and Rosemary Radford Ruether (Bloomington and Indianapolis: Indiana University Press, 2006), 11–23.
4. Nauvoo Relief Society Minute Book, April 28, 1842, *The Joseph Smith Papers,* 40, http://www.josephsmithpapers.org/paper-summary/nauvoo-relief-society-minute-book/37.

# Stay and Help Us Change

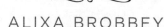

## ALIXA BROBBEY

Alixa Brobbey was born and raised in the Netherlands. She lived in Ghana for two years before traveling to study English at Brigham Young University, Provo, Utah. She's grateful for her goodly parents and loving younger sisters, the gospel, and the opportunity to call three different countries home. Her mother is Alice Brobbey, whose essay also appears in this volume.

Once, when I was a little girl growing up in the Netherlands, a man from South Africa visited our branch and stood up to share his testimony. I can't remember many specific things I heard at the pulpit in that little red-brick building, but I do recall that as this man was speaking, he remarked on how interesting it was to see white and black members of the Church worshipping together in the same room. I can recall that the congregation seemed to simultaneously hold their breath and try to inconspicuously glance back at my family to see how we handled his comment. Now, as an adult, I understand that this aspect of his testimony had more to do with the effects of apartheid than with anything concerning the doctrine of The Church of Jesus Christ of Latter-day Saints. But as a child, all I felt was a stinging, hot sensation on my cheeks. We were the only Black family in our congregation, and that day I wondered if we were so different, we should leave and find somewhere else to practice our religion.

As I continued to age and progress in the Church, I had several more experiences in which someone else's personal culture, history, or views made me question whether or not a church whose stereotypical leaders are older, white, American, conservative males had a place for me. During an activity for Young Women, shortly after United States president Barack Obama was reelected, one of my American Young

Women leaders in the Netherlands unexpectedly vented to us girls about how upset she was. She claimed that the results showed that America's values were eroding. She warned us about the times we were living in and alluded to a personal belief that her nation's new leader was an anti-Christ. I was confused. I mused at her inappropriately sharing personal opinions in such a setting. Those expressions had nothing to do with the true gospel. My parents, both active Church members, had celebrated Obama's victory as a sign of progress. We were excited that the so-called leader of the free world looked like us. At thirteen years old, I had not yet developed my political opinions, and listening to my leader's tirade made me wonder if I could have liberal views and still be considered a good Latter-day Saint.

During seminary class a few years later, my teacher complained that diversity quotas were making it difficult for people like him in the job market. He told us that no matter how qualified white men like him were, they now always lost jobs and promotions to ethnic minorities and women. This was not presented as a topic for debate or discussion. He presented it simply as somebody with more experience telling the younger generation facts about life. Once again, an issue that had little to do with doctrine was discussed in a church setting and caused me great discomfort. Listening to him speak, I disagreed strongly with his argument but did not know how to raise my hand and challenge a priesthood holder during a Church-sponsored meeting. I tried to ignore his words and focus on the message of his lesson, but all these years later I cannot recall what scriptural message he taught us that day. I do recall, however, how alone I felt when nobody challenged him. And I wondered whether, in a class of about eight, he even registered that I was there. Surely, he would not have said such things if he'd remembered I was in the room?

Despite these events, I tried to focus on the essence of the gospel. That helped me to continue to attend church despite negative experiences, which were the deviation rather than the norm. I was blessed with many leaders and teachers who greatly strengthened my testimony and helped me to learn. My parents taught me that I go to church because of what I believe, not because of who is there. Their counsel was a great blessing when things were difficult. I continued studying the scriptures daily, I went to Mutual activities and completed my Personal Progress program, and even when it was early and dark and I didn't feel like going, I hopped on my bike and rode to seminary. I began to learn the importance of separating the doctrine of the Church from aspects of its culture.

During this time, I grew to love reading the *New Era*. When I was growing up, I always dreamt about being a writer, and so as soon as I found out how to, I worked on composing and submitting a piece for the monthly Church magazine for teens. When my piece was chosen for publication, the editors asked me for a photo. I sent them one of me, with my brown eyes and black hair braided in cornrows. When the story was finally published, the accompanying illustration was one of a girl with blonde hair and blue eyes. I tell that story to my friends now, laughing about how different I look in the magazine compared to in real life. Despite seeing the funny side, however, I realize that this story shows that even though there are many Latter-day Saints all over the world, many of us feel like we have to strive for some sort of successful Utah Mormon Mom Blogger ideal.

Ironically, it was the place I least expected that helped me come to terms with the fact that I don't necessarily look, think, speak, or act like other Church members. Throughout my first years of high school, I resented the thought of attending Brigham Young University. The thought of being surrounded by people who shared some of the same biases, assumptions, and sometimes demeaning cultural beliefs I'd experienced as a child seemed a little nauseating. However, during my junior year, moving to Ghana gave me the chance to develop my personal relationship with my Savior. I began to look at BYU's positive aspects and discovered that there was a lot about the university to like. While working with me on my college applications, my guidance counselor looked up statistics on BYU and asked me if I really wanted to move to a place where only 1 percent of the student body shared my ethnicity. When I told her that I'd grown up around mostly white people in Europe, she warned me that white Americans were very different. Though I was still hesitant, I prayerfully determined that going to school in Provo, Utah, would be the best choice for me at that time. Attending BYU turned out to be a wonderful blessing.

Although I've had moments in which people were insensitive, naïvely unkind, or even openly hostile, it was there I discovered that unlike what I had thought growing up, there are a myriad of ways to be a Latter-day Saint. Within the culture of Christ, there are so many ways to be a woman of God. My friends, roommates, mentors, and strangers have shown me that living the gospel isn't a one-size-fits-all exercise. My friend who registered as a Democrat as soon as she turned eighteen showed me this. My roommate who identifies as asexual and opened up to me about trying to reconcile this with a desire for a temple marriage showed me this. My professor who chose not to take her husband's last name and taught full-time while raising young children showed me this. My resident assistant (RA) with her pixie cut and cat sweaters, my roommate who worried that eating disorders would prevent her from being a good missionary, and my coworkers who are well into their twenties but have never had boyfriends all show me this. By the way women around me continue to live the gospel faithfully, despite their trials and differences, I gain the courage to continue to come to church and to Jesus Christ as I am.

Recently, I went to an event sponsored by the BYU Black Alumni Society. While getting to know each other and sharing our experiences, we ended up discussing the lack of representation we sometimes feel. Rhonda Peck, BYU Law Student Bar Association president, encouraged us to see her as a mentor. She said that she was initially skeptical about attending a school where few people were multiracial like her. She shared with us an observation she had made at a student luncheon when she asked the professor next to her, "Where is the diversity in this room?" Providentially, he invited her to "come, and help us make it better."

I think we can take a similar approach with our fellow members in the Church. The people within it are not perfect. Sometimes it feels easier to give up and stay away than to attend meetings and activities in which we may feel that our voices are not heard. I've learned, though, that things cannot get better unless we are in the room sharing our ideas and advocating for ourselves and others like us. Let us continue to share our light, our stories, our pains and triumphs so that others may be comforted by them as they strive to find their place within the Church. Rather than turning away, may we all have the strength to stay and help those around us become more loving, open, and welcoming while we journey to become more like the Savior.

# Family Fabric

## JILL MULVAY DERR

Melese Spaulding Miller

Jill Mulvay Derr has studied the history of Latter-day Saint women for more than four decades. She was an associate professor and later managing director of the Joseph Fielding Smith Institute for Church History at Brigham Young University, Provo, Utah. The author of many scholarly works, she coedited *The First Fifty Years of Relief Society: Key Documents in Latter-day Saint Women's History.* She and her husband, C. Brooklyn Derr, are the parents of four children and have eleven grandchildren.

My two sisters and I always fled when our Uncle Kenneth came to visit. At the first sound of his booming voice, we ran down the hall to our bedroom closet, squashed ourselves against hanging dresses, and pulled shut the sliding door. Then we squealed and laughed until we'd finished our fun and went out to greet our great-uncle—brother of our deceased maternal grandmother and our two beloved great-aunts. Kenneth was a big man—tall and broad—who had married shortly after completing his service in a World War I cavalry unit, quickly divorced, and married a second time to a Swedish immigrant nine years his senior. Kenneth outlived her by three decades. I remember him for his fish stories and boisterous banter—the silly jokes and shady jokes punctuated with quips about our loveliness and the supposedly eager young suitors our parents would have to beat off with a stick. Kenneth had no children of his own.

My parents had four children—three daughters and a son. Not until years later would I consider the possibility that my mother's childless aunts and uncle might long to be around children. Certainly "the Aunts" treated my mother and her four sisters as daughters, all the more so following my grandmother's early death. Those two white-haired women born in the 1880s were the matriarchs of our family. They hosted Sunday and holiday dinners, lent money and advice, and gave away their crab apple jelly, raspberry starts, and land. Well into the 1950s, they maintained ties to their father's homestead in Big Cottonwood Canyon, working beside their husbands to run a rustic lodge and restaurant on the old creek-side property. After retiring they traveled abroad, but travel only reaffirmed their loyalty to Utah's mountains and valleys—the land settled by their Mormon pioneer ancestors.

Neither the Aunts nor Kenneth were Latter-day Saints. Their parents had severed ties with the Church when they married in 1878. As family lore has it, at age nineteen, Richard swept sixteen-year-old Mary onto the back of his horse, and they eloped, escaping whispered possibilities of plural marriage and definitively forsaking Mormonism.[1] The eight children born to Richard and Mary harbored hostility toward the Saints that was passed along to their children and grandchildren. My mother, with her mother and four sisters, attended the Baptist church. My grandfather came to Utah from New Jersey having fully absorbed anti-Mormon tracts. After my grandmother's death, he followed Christian Science and the United Church of Christ. The Aunts, like most of Richard and Mary's children and grandchildren, were believing Christians but not churchgoers.

My father's pioneer heritage came through his mother, a proud member of Daughters of Utah Pioneers, and he was baptized a Latter-day Saint at eight years of age. But his stint with the Navy during World War II distanced him from the Church, and he promised my mother when they married that he would not be a member of the Church. Thus my siblings and I were descended from pioneer stock but did not grow up in a Latter-day Saint family. When we entered elementary school in our new neighborhood south of Salt Lake City, my mother and father thought Church association would help us make friends, and so they allowed us to attend Primary and Sunday School (the latter presided over by Sister Angell!). In that sense, we were not much different from many of our neighbors and schoolmates who came from heterodox families but often attended Church functions.

When my older sister approached her eighth birthday and expressed her desire to be baptized a member of The Church of Jesus Christ of Latter-day Saints, conflict over religion became a cloud that hovered above our family life. My parents urged my sister to wait until she was sixteen, but some twenty months later they relented, and she and I were baptized on the same day in the old font at the Salt Lake Tabernacle. My younger sister and brother followed suit with my parents' consent. Having embraced choice and love as their primary values, my mother and father supported us as we attended Sunday meetings and Primary and then Mutual and seminary activities. The extended family turned out en masse when my brother left on his mission.

Still, differing religious beliefs and practices did not disappear, and I played my own role in exacerbating divisions. I told my mother I could not be entirely happy unless she was baptized a Latter-day Saint; I boycotted Easter Sunday brunch when the extended family gathered that day at a restaurant; I took bottles of gin from the kitchen cupboard, poured the liquor down the drain, and refilled the bottles with water. Much of my youthful knowledge of the gospel of Jesus Christ centered on its rules and standards, and I was better acquainted with the letter of the law than the spirit of the law, or for that matter, the Spirit. I loved, honored, and obeyed my parents, and we shared thousands of joyful moments. Yet, in egregious and in subtle ways I treated them as outsiders.

My mother sewed wedding dresses for each of her three daughters in turn and then waited outside the temple three times, unable to witness any one of them exchange her marriage vows. Conflict and pain shadowed these occasions, and I still ask myself in what ways it might have played out differently. Acknowledging and accepting differences in values and belief does not eliminate them. Across ensuing years I prayed for the charity I needed to empathize with my parents' hurts and bridge the spoken and unspoken distances between us. They may have uttered their own prayers because their hearts continued to soften. As their posterity increased, my father and mother stepped forward again and again to show respect for our religious commitments. They attended nearly two dozen baptisms for their grandchildren and various missionary farewells and homecomings—cheerfully joining in the singing of hymns. On numerous occasions they patiently listened to me present talks and papers on the history of Latter-day Saint women. They consistently honored my choices and expected me to honor theirs.

In the late 1980s, as I was researching and writing Relief Society history, I chatted one day with a member of the Relief Society General Board. We shared family news and plans for the upcoming holiday. I told her that at gatherings of my extended family there were usually two punch bowls—one with liquor and one without. She expressed surprise and sympathy. "I'm so sorry for you," she said, and her statement surprised me. Sorry for me?

It might not have been the first time I recognized my appreciation for my unorthodox family, but it became a moment that marked gratitude for the tolerance and respect we had come to share. Across the years my extended family opened my eyes to such troubles as divorce, bankruptcy, alcoholism, and suicide. Of course, those difficulties spread themselves across families of all faiths, but such realities counterbalanced the "model" Latter-day Saint family I had so long hoped for. I was nearing thirty when I married a remarkable man (recently divorced), inherited his son and two daughters, and then added a son. We did not exactly fit the traditional mold, but my expectations for such a fit had ebbed.

Gradually, instead of seeing all that separated my family of origin and my church, I came to see the Church as an extension of that family—a collection of women and men often as flawed as they are gifted. I can run, hide, or scoff when hard-to-understand characters like my Uncle Kenneth appear on the scene. Ultimately, however, I have to come to terms with those I do not understand, whether they are part of the Latter-day Saint past or present, leaders or rank-and-file members, seekers or dissidents. This remains an ongoing process for me, a series of heart changes, not a single transformative epiphany. When I first encountered some of Brigham Young's harsh statements concerning women, I was shocked and angry. Closer encounters with Brigham's thought, family, leadership, and capacity for growth tempered my initial reaction, and I developed appreciation and even affection for the man. Similarly, it has taken me years first to accept friends who declared themselves to be gays or lesbians and then more years to respect their committed partnerships and marriages and acknowledge their happiness.

The Lord has admonished us to "be ashamed . . . of all [our] littleness of soul" (Doctrine and Covenants 117:11). "Away with self-righteousness," Joseph Smith taught sisters of the Female Relief Society of Nauvoo. Rather, he counseled, "You must enlarge your souls towards others if you would do like Jesus, and carry your fellow creatures to Abram's bosom."[2] There may be some for whom that enlargement of soul comes naturally or easily or speedily, but not for me. Over time I have learned to fight my own rushes to judgment. To obey God's laws because we love the Lawgiver: that is the sure way to become humble and not contracted in feeling or inclined to "hide" ourselves from our "own flesh" (Isaiah 58:7). We all live with dissonances as imperfect people struggle to live divine law, and we become Saints as soulful covenant-keeping deepens our compassion, heightens harmony, and strengthens the family fabric across generations and through eternity.

## NOTES

1. In fact, Mary's parents had decided to join those called to Arizona to establish a Latter-day Saint settlement there, and Richard "literally took Mary out of the wagon" as they were about to leave. Family reminiscence in author's possession.

2. "A Book of Records Containing the proceedings of The Female Relief Society of Nauvoo," April 28 and June 9, 1842, in *The First Fifty Years of Relief Society: Key Documents in Latter-day Saint Women's History*, edited by Jill Mulvay Derr, Carol Cornwall Madsen, Kate Holbrook, and Matthew J. Grow (Salt Lake City: Church Historian's Press, 2016), 58, 79; spelling standardized.

# UNITY IN SISTERHOOD

We are part of a grand whole. We need each
other to make our sisterhood complete.

—*Elaine L. Jack*

# Stay Connected to Your Roots

## LASHAWN WILLIAMS

Dr. LaShawn Williams is a licensed clinical social worker (LCSW) and member of the faculty at Utah Valley University, Orem, Utah. She is a divorced parent of three small humans and strives to teach them their divine existences in an intentional way.

Hey, Sis,

I honestly wasn't sure I had anything beneficial to put into words about this journey for Black women in a church that struggles to demonstrate how we all are alike unto God without having to be exactly the same type of person. I was reminded of Ada Maria Isasi-Diaz's words, speaking of our Latina sisters in the Christian faith, when she says, "How can I say what Latinas believe so the churches will minister to us and with us, not change us into the kind of Christians the institutional churches want, but to encourage us to put our beliefs ever more into action?"[1] The older I've gotten, this is, comparatively, what I've wondered for my sisters in the Black African diaspora. How do I share who we are and what we believe? How do I help sisters know that they can come as they are and that through us and our deep, abiding faith in Christ, we can—and are supported to—put our beliefs into action, both in ourselves and in our communities?

It's a conversation our non-Black sisters are having as well—feeling as though their myriad identities belong in our shared spaces and yet are often marginalized. We are not alone. We are all seeking to be seen as valued and valuable for the many layers and pieces that make us diverse women of godly heritage. Additionally, we have our histories to grapple with. It's a tall order to define, understand, and possibly redefine yourself within the space of deep faith. Yet, I know just as deeply that we desire to be whole and to be well.

Still, I wondered what I could tell you to help you know that you belong here, just as you are. Our wonderful, timely, thoughtful, believing, lovely, and faithful God, through the reach and connection of and to our ancestors, inspired me, as He always does, to remember that it is important to tell our own parts of our faith family's story. Our part of this story is what happens when women decide that they belong. By decide, I mean to assert oneself in a particular place and time. In our case, it was asserting our visibility in the history, present, and future of our faith and our membership in The Church of Jesus Christ of Latter-day Saints.

We knew that this space was created for us, even if our present experiences seemed to illustrate that our various ward families were experiencing long-term cases of amnesia, lack of vision, and hearing loss. It was painful. They couldn't remember our literal and spiritual pioneer stories as easily as we remembered theirs. It seemed they couldn't see us where we stood, even when it was next to them. They didn't appear to hear us share our truths. And if there is anything we know about being called to stand as witnesses of God and to do His work where we stand, it is that we must have ears to hear, eyes to see, clear minds, and pure hearts. There were times within my sister group that we felt our engagement at church was blocked by blind, deaf, stiff-necked siblings who refused to bend to the influence of the Spirit enough to hear their sisters in Christ.

As a result, some of our sisters left. Some took breaks in attendance and engagement. Those of us who stayed checked in with each other and held space for each other. We talked and cried and wondered and questioned. We did it with each other and for each other. When some of us could watch general conference and others of us couldn't because it felt suffocating, we simply made space for one another to sit, stand, and rest in the truth of her experience. Some of us could attend the temple. Some of us could no longer bear not seeing ourselves, our experiences, or faces like ours in our sacred spaces, and so we chose not to attend. Yet all the while, we continued to choose each other.

That is the important part.

We chose each other because we remembered that our Savior

chooses us. Every time. No matter what. It was in 2013 when events in the United States criminal justice system caused my sister friends and I to be on the phone together and in tears. We were discussing our struggles at church, in the Church, and sometimes because of the Church. This time was the first of what would become many conversations over the course of a few years before we understood our path. Once we understood it, we felt our strength grow in the worship of Christ through our membership in this Church. Until we reached that point, we asked questions that we couldn't sufficiently answer for each other. There were times that we wondered if the Church as a worldwide institution cared about social issues affecting the Black community in the United States.

Wading through seemingly unrelenting injustices is a process. What I can tell you is that we can never give up on one another, or on God, or in our ability to find God's word as directed to us. We heard God in one another's testimonies and tears. We heard God through some of our leaders from the past and the present, both inside and outside the Church. General conference in October 2013 was a shift for us. Elder Dieter F. Uchtdorf gave a talk that was one of the moments in which we felt both heard and seen: "And, to be perfectly frank, there have been times when members or leaders in the Church have simply made mistakes. There may have been things said or done that were not in harmony with our values, principles, or doctrine. I suppose the Church would be perfect only if it were run by perfect beings. God is perfect, and His doctrine is pure. But He works through us—His imperfect children—and imperfect people make mistakes."[2]

We knew Elder Uchtdorf couldn't be the only one brave enough to admit that previous leaders had made mistakes and that the Church isn't perfect. We wondered who else demonstrated similar bravery that we could discover. We knew the leaders were not perfect. We didn't expect them to be. In our research we found Hugh B. Brown, Stephen Taggart, Lowry Nelson, and Linda K. Newell who were particularly sensitive to our plight. We found non-Black men and women who attempted to stand in the gaps for their Black brothers and sisters. We then wondered what, if anything, we could do to make the Church a place with expanded vision? A church that could see and celebrate our cultural bravery too? Because as much as white scholars study the Black experience, they can relate only up to a certain point. They lack the nuances of lived experience that only we, as Black people, can provide.

One evening, after hosting a gathering of Black Latter-day Saint college students one weekend, we asked, "What if we had a pageant for Black history in the Church?" We knew the stories of Green Flake, Jane Manning James, Elijah Abel, Sam and Amanda Chambers, the Martins family, and others. But did our fellow Saints? We recognized that feeling invisible in our own faith home was because our brothers and sisters didn't know our stories the way we knew theirs. So, we took out markers and a sister's trusty planner-journal, and started drafting a pageant. We realized, as Black women born and raised in the United States, that there had never been a story of Black Latter-day Saints that connected with the Black African diaspora. Our faith in the restored gospel informed our focus on restoring the various Black cultures as a connected people through the gospel of our faith. Our pageant idea rooted us in continental Africa and through the effects of the transatlantic slave trade, told the story of God's Black children throughout the world who found their spiritual home in The Church of Jesus Christ. We linked Africa to South America, to the Caribbean, and to the U.S. to find and tell the stories of our brothers and sisters who made a way to survive the horrors of enslavement. We wanted to share the stories of Saints who persevered and who motivated us to continue to persevere. We knew that connecting ourselves to our roots would help us connect to each other. As we connected with each other, we became a force for other Black Saints to connect as well. We felt that our pioneer ancestors were guiding us in this work to tell of their journeys and speak to their presence from the center and not the sidelines. We didn't know if the Church would agree to a pageant, but we dared to find a way to ask that they consider it in 2018—the fortieth anniversary of the revelation extending priesthood to Black members of the Church.

As we prayed over our pageant, we were invited to do groundwork and develop what has become our ministry: sharing and preserving the legacy of Black Latter-day Saints. We found ourselves working through our sister friend's public relations calling in the Washington, D.C., area to create the first ever Black LDS Legacy conference in February 2018. More than nine hundred people attended the Washington D.C. Temple Visitors' Center to learn and celebrate the history of Black people who pioneered their own way in the Church.[3] All of our speakers were Black. All of our topics were centered on Black experiences in the Church with scripture study, identity work, women's work, and missionary and temple work. There were reflections that helped to show how resistance is a way forward in faith. We invited all Saints to see, experience, and celebrate the world through our lens as Black people. We prayed in the tradition of our historical Black churches, we opened our conference with the "Amen" chorus and ended with the Black anthem, "Lift Every Voice and Sing." As we welcomed participants from up and down the eastern seaboard and online via social media, the presence of our ancestors was palpable. We were present. We were rooted in them, and they were present in us. We were lifted by them, and in turn we were able to lift others. What started as one conference has grown into three. Additional invitations have been received to bring the conference to many cities in the U.S. The conference was covered by the *Church News* and deemed "historical." We were grateful and humbled and emboldened.

Our ancestors did not let us rest. After the D.C. conference, we thought our pageant might really happen. We dreamt big and we dreamt bold. Not only did we want it to happen but we wanted it to happen in the Conference Center in Salt Lake City. We wanted all Black people of the African diaspora to be represented on stage and no white people—with the exception of a member of the Quorum of the Twelve Apostles. But remember, we were bold, so we changed that exception to be only a member of the First Presidency! We wanted to pitch our biggest, boldest, and Blackest ideas to Church leadership and dared their love for us to shine through as we'd never seen or experienced it to date. Would the Lord show us He had heard our prayers and supplications and tears and trials?

The leaders of the Church not only approved the draft of our pageant but added to it with our support, input, and approval at every step. The June 1, 2018 "Be One" event was born . . . to take place in the Conference Center (check!) with all Black performers and narrators (check!) and almost no white people . . . except for our prophet and President, Russell M. Nelson, and a member of the First Presidency (CHECK! CHECK! CHECK! CELESTIAL GOLD STAR!). As we sat in the audience watching our pageant come to life, we cried. We were seeing our people, our stories, and our histories in our faith. And we rejoiced because we saw that this is what can happen when we assert our identity in our place of faith, when we choose to worship Christ in the spirit of our ancestors, and step into our ministry as the bold, beautiful, blessed, and highly favored people that we are.

The pageant process was not easy by any means, but most missionary work isn't. We gained deeper testimonies of God's love for us through his imperfect but willing servants. If you had told us in 2013 that we could make bold requests in the tradition of prayer circles of our families/ancestors and that God would say yes at every turn, we would have laughed.[4] But it is exactly those questions, those cultural and spiritual ransoms that we laid at the altar and our Heavenly Parents saw fit to answer. In doing so They have equipped us to continue to do this work with and for our people inside and outside the Black community. Our conferences and the pageant were just the beginning. We continue working to create the space we need in order to experience the connection, affirmation, and healing that we want. We learned that we weren't the only ones who needed it. So wherever you are, dear sister, if you are in need of healing and hope—let our story show you that God will help you create it. You, as beautiful, blessed, and Black as you are, belong! Come as you are. Stay connected to your roots. We are who we've been waiting for. We are arriving.

## NOTES

1. Ada Maria Isasi-Diaz, *Mujerista Theology: A Theology for the Twenty-First Century* (Maryknoll, NY: Orbis Books, 2013), 4.
2. Dieter F. Uchtdorf, "Come, Join with Us," *Ensign*, November 2013.
3. Page Johnson, "Historic Conference in Washington, D.C., Discusses the 'Legacy of Black LDS Pioneers,'" *Deseret News*, February 23, 2018, https://www.thechurchnews.com/archive/2018–02–21/historic-conference-in-washington-d-c-discusses-the-legacy-of-black-lds-pioneers-33374.
4. In Black families, we hold hands with each other when we pray. This practice extended to our planning committee for the "Be One" event.

# Acts of Creation

## MELISSA MASON

Melissa Mason lives in southern California with her husband and four children. She served as director of Claremont Graduate University's Mormon Women's Oral History Project and is the founder of Claremont Canopy, a nonprofit organization that helps locally resettled refugees thrive in their new communities. She enjoys designing modern quilts, being politically active, and yelling at people on Twitter.

Amy Barrett

We are scattered around the living room of a mountain lodge, snuggled under blankets, quietly grazing on chocolates while stuffed deer heads stare down at us in judgment. Sitting attentively, fifteen of us listen to Allyson tell stories of herself as a young, wild girl riding horses through the mountains, growing up, finding her voice. She speaks and we listen and on the rustic log coffee table a little recorder captures it all. The stories she tells, the stories we all will tell that weekend, will not float untethered in the ether of our memories but will be preserved. Preserved for what, we do not know. We are gathered not only for what is being created but also for the act of creation itself.

Although we met in our twenties, I don't think it's wrong to say that many of us grew up in our faith together. This motley little group first assembled over the course of several years in the South Bend Ward in Indiana. Most of the husbands were working on doctorates, and most of the wives were home with babies and toddlers. It was an intense crucible of exams and diapers and job searches and postpartum depression through which we were forged individually and together. We spent mornings at the Burger King playground and evenings in our living rooms, talking endlessly about all that we had on our plates, our responsibilities and our anxieties with our faith and practice ever looming over it all.

The years passed quickly, and then in a short time we all began to scatter, like leaves that have settled on the ground and are then blown apart by a strong gust. We landed all over the country—California, Oregon, Utah, Colorado, New York, connected only by email updates.

There's a security in being around people who know you well. A sense of being seen. The South Bend Ward was a welcoming place. In this rust belt town on the Michigan-Indiana border, members held onto their community tightly, careful not to take it for granted. Unlike wards I've attended elsewhere where it was easy to get lost in the crowd, in South Bend there was a general feeling of "we're just glad you're here." Still trying to quit smoking? Grab a pew. Burly Hell's Angel? Congrats, you're the new elders quorum president. Wearing pants rather than a skirt? It's too dang cold for skirts anyway; here's the sign-up for the chili cook-off. I'd heard tales of the stereotypical Molly Mormon, but rarely had I glimpsed her in the wilds of those early years of my Church membership. Instead, we all showed up to church as we were and got to work.

Perhaps it was unfortunate that the first ward I had ever been a part of was the South Bend Ward because I have spent the years since searching for it wherever I go. The group of us who shared that experience had come to rest far from one another, and more than one reported the feeling of being unknown in their new home, their new ward. Permeating our emails to each other was a sense of loneliness and displacement.

As Latter-day Saint women, we take our cues from other women in the Church. We can validate and reinforce each other's quirks and oddities. We can also quash and cast suspicion on one another when something is different or outside the norm. Which behaviors dominate in any particular ward or community is a game of roulette. Unfortunately, many of us found ourselves in places where we began to see a mold that we existed outside of. It's not difficult to see how that path can lead to self-doubt, loneliness, and isolation, real or perceived.

Around this time, I became involved in the Mormon Women's Oral History Project sponsored by Claremont Graduate University, which records and preserves women's stories for the historical record. There is something transformative about individuals unfolding their life story in front of you. Think of the women you know in a two-dimensional way: the grandmother whose life you know only the basic details about, the sister who sits in the back row in Relief Society, the perfectly put-together supermom Primary president. Knowing their stories, they suddenly become persons whose thoughts, feelings, and experiences are as full and complex as yours. Do enough of these interviews, and the idea that there is any single way to be a Latter-day Saint woman becomes a joke. If we do indeed take our cues from other women in the Church, then the possibilities of who we can be are limitless. We just need to be sure that we're listening to enough voices to glimpse the diversity. Luckily for us, the Church provides us the social space to encounter one another. It is our imperative to get creative and expand or dispel the limits of the categories we neatly place each other into.

Amid these discussions we were having in our emails, we realized that we needed to learn to listen to and validate our own voices, our own stories, first. We formed an online discussion group to figure out what our individual, lived "Mormonisms" looked like. We centered ourselves on the syllabus my husband had created for a class he was teaching fall semester 2012 through spring 2013 entitled "Gendering Mormonism." Over the course of a year, we would critically examine our faith tradition informed by academic readings and the crucial lenses of our own experiences. We covered feminism, sexuality, patriarchy, polygamy, modern Latter-day Saint women's experiences, the priesthood, and the temple, among many other topics. With each lesson, we absorbed and wrestled and talked through and refined our thoughts and beliefs. We honed our faith. We became comfortable with our voices.

At the end of that year, we finally came together at that mountain lodge and began to speak. Having learned to give structure to our thoughts and feelings in our discussions, we felt more confident that we each had an individual voice that was unique, relevant, and needed to be heard. The stories we told didn't proverbially paint a picture of the speaker; instead they sculpted a multidimensional, dynamic individual. To speak through the experiences that formed us, the questions that stumped us, to give life to what existed only in our minds was transformative, empowering, and creative. We stood as witnesses for each other and for ourselves. We recorded those stories and archived them for others to listen to.

The idea of cramming such complex and beautiful beings into a mold now seems laughable. To toss out the myth of that mold and give ourselves the freedom to explore our faith, to honestly seek, whether we find answers or not, allowed us each to look at who we are, what has made us, what we are capable of. It hasn't solved all our problems or ameliorated our discomforts. Those have continued to be a part of the journey of many of us. But it has altered our approaches to those journeys and taught us to be kind and patient with ourselves and others as we progress and constantly re-create what it means to be a woman of faith. And that feels divine.

# Of Solar Eclipses
# and Circles of Belonging
## Finding Inclusion out of Exclusion

## ANDREA G. RADKE-MOSS

Andrea G. Radke-Moss is a professor of history at Brigham Young University–Idaho, Rexburg, Idaho. She is the author of *Bright Epoch*, a history of female students at land-grant colleges in the nineteenth-century American West. She has researched and written on many topics related to Latter-day Saint women's experiences and lives in Rexburg with her husband and two children.

On August 21, 2017, our Idaho community was one of hundreds across America that experienced the total solar eclipse. My children and I sat waiting with our friends in the backyard, periodically looking through our eclipse glasses while the moon's disc inched its way over the sun. Finally, those anticipated two and a half minutes arrived: the shadow of the moon passed from west to east across the earth and encompassed us all in its cool gloaming. But it was only at that moment of total contact between the two competing spheres, when the moon completely covered the sun, that the greatest magic was revealed: the corona of sun flares leaped out from their lunar curtain in pointed ribbons of light; and then, the diamond ring of concentrated brilliance peeked from behind one spot on the moon's uneven surface. Both the corona and the diamond ring are visible only in the darkness of a total solar eclipse and only for a few moments. A chorus of gasps, cheers, laughter, and tears rang out from the backyards across our neighborhood and our community, uniting thousands of people in a moment of celestial transcendence. There was no fear or confusion, only peace, humility, and wonder. I have since considered how sometimes the wholeness of true community occurs when seemingly opposing or contradictory forces come together, like those two spheres—rarely seen together at the same time—which joined in the high summer sky and covered everyone in a circle of beautiful belonging.

Some of my earliest memories are related to feeling as if I did not fit into various circles of inclusion. As a child who was shy, sensitive, and often socially awkward, public interactions felt intimidating and unnatural, even with older siblings and cousins, leaving me to feel as if I were observing from the sidelines. Still, I had a happy and secure childhood, raised in the confidence of the love of God and my family. On one occasion, at eleven years old, I remember sitting in a desk feeling particularly alone and then saying a short prayer in my head for comfort. At that moment, an overwhelming sensation of love and warmth washed over me, assuring me that my Heavenly Parents were aware of me and loved me, bringing me into a circle of comforting reassurance. At times I've stepped outside that circle because of doubts, fear, or lost confidence, but it's always there, welcoming me back when I return to it. My earthly parents had accepted a new faith tradition as a young married couple, on their own and without the support of extended family, most of whom did not accept their religious choice. Still, they raised their family devotedly in the gospel of Jesus Christ. They modeled what it meant to sit on the edges of their old circles, even while drawing new ones around their children, church, and community, through love, faith, and service.

I similarly knew how it felt to be outside of circles. I was the only member of the Church in my school, and my family was among only a few members of the Church in our town and extended relations. We often stood outside. But I also felt the difference of not really belonging within my faith community. For example, I didn't receive my Young Womanhood Recognition Award, nor did I graduate from seminary. I succeeded academically in college, but I struggled miserably at dating. I watched as friend after friend married and I didn't. I did not serve a mission until I was twenty-four years old. I became a Relief Society president as an unmarried graduate student. I pursued a doctorate and followed an academic career path. I married at age thirty-four, long after I considered that choice outside of my reach. And I found myself a new mother at an age when most of my peers already had children graduating from high school. My life involved very few of the expected life milestones for a Latter-day Saint female, and they definitely were not in the "right order." But along the way, I managed to create new circles, with different expectations of what it meant to be a faithful woman, and then I endeavored to bring my friends, new converts, and college students into those circles of inclusion. Now I am a full-time professor, a historian, a wife, an older mother of young children, a Church member, and a feminist—a combination that sometimes leaves me sitting on the margins of many circles.

Whether real or perceived, internally felt or externally imposed, our differences too often place us at odds with our various communities. But they don't have to, for "in the spiritual realm, diversity is the glorious equation of difference coupled with loyalty and commitment."[1] This observation reminds me of Paul's great metaphor of the body of Christ, in which "the body is one, and hath many members, and all members of that one body, being many, are one body: so also is Christ" (1 Corinthians 12:12). We also call this Zion, or the "pure in heart," who are living with "one heart and one mind" (Moses 7:18). Some see Zion as a place, like a "family" or the "kingdom of God"; others see it as a "refuge," a "big tent," or as "circles of inclusion," as I am suggesting here, all of which involve somewhat permeable boundaries through which its members come and go. We know that differences should be embraced in this process of making Zion, but that is not an easy reality for those who stand outside full acceptance in the Church. For example, feminists like me struggle with desires for a greater gender parity that might be seen as dissonant with more traditional views. While some of these voices seek to "advocat[e] for some changes while maintaining loyalty to the institutional church," others are "resisting the pressure to mold the church to fit new belief about gender."[2] The result is sometimes catastrophic collisions within the body of Christ, leading to "harsh comments, invitations to leave the church, and comparisons to history's worst moments."[3] Even expressions of pain over gender inequality are dismissed as irrelevant or as indicators of a lack of faith. But since "mourning with those that mourn" is a condition of Zion, charity means "not dismissing others' pain simply because we do not feel it ourselves."[4]

Is it any wonder then, that in expressing differences in ideas, we believe that we are isolated or that our differences are not even wanted or needed in the body of Christ? Like the foot, who considers his own unimportance and asks, "Because I am not the hand, . . . is it therefore not of the body?" (1 Corinthians 12:15), I have also wondered, "Is there a place for me?" Rather than cutting off those members "which seem to be more feeble" (1 Corinthians 12:21–22), we should remember that others in our body of Christ have struggled even more for inclusion, perhaps because of racial differences, faith challenges, sexual identity or orientation, economic status, health problems, cultural variances, or different mental or physical abilities.[5] Or perhaps our fellow Saints are in pain simply because they are not ready for the changes happening in the Church on some of these issues. As I have said elsewhere, the Church is not moving as fast as many of us would like, but it is also moving at a blistering pace for others. Can we have charity for both? Both speeds come with great discomfort for those on the journey.[6] Just as I want charity extended to me for desiring more change, I must offer the same charity to those who are cautious of change.

Although I sometimes feel unsure of my place within the body of Christ, I have felt the Spirit guide me to those in need of welcome into the Lord's circles of inclusion. This has involved at times nurturing students who are grappling with doubt, seemingly unanswerable questions, and other intellectual trials of faith, or just lack of academic confidence and success. But it also means listening to and loving those who cope with divorce, infertility, sexual identity, loneliness, depression, racism, or sexual assault. I have at times felt like a toenail, on the farthest extremes of our body of Christ. But I have also felt like the very heart of the body, beating to keep myself and other members alive. Remember Edwin Markham's famous poem:

> *He drew a circle that shut me out—*
> *Heretic, rebel, a thing to flout*
> *But love and I had the wit to win:*
> *We drew a circle and took him in!*[7]

And that is the irony—the very things that might keep us out of some circles of our religious fellowship are the very things needed for pulling others back in.

Funny how it seems so much easier to dwell on the times when you have felt excluded, but it's not as easy to remember when you have been included. And yet, those merciful moments have happened to me, often when I least expected it, thus following Paul's encouragement "that there should be no schism in the body; . . . And whether one member suffer, all the members suffer with it; or one member be honoured, all the members rejoice with it" (1 Corinthians 12:25–26). Like when I nervously wore pants to church in December of 2012, a Church friend approached me, cheerfully looked me up and down, and said, "Oh! Feminist Sunday! You look great." And after a hard discussion in one Church lesson, a woman took me aside and said, "This must be a difficult topic for you. But I want you to know that I appreciate your perspective, and I'm glad that you're you." And in another period of personal searching, all it took to lift my heart was for a priesthood leader to say, "I know you struggle with this issue. I don't have an answer for you, but I encourage you to hang in there and keep hope alive." No judgment, no patronizing answers, only listening and empathy. In January of 2016, I attended the Women's March on Washington with a group of other feminist Latter-day Saint women, and I was nervous to put myself on the line so publicly, especially when I assumed that most people in my community would disagree with my action. But one neighbor woman met me at the end of our shared driveways and said, "I think it's wonderful that you get to go and have the opportunity to stand up for what is important to you." No condemnation, only support. I cherish these examples of disciples of Christ drawing their circles wide for me.

Although feelings of exclusion have sometimes crippled me, they have also pushed me to draw new circles for others. Even my faith and feminism have collided in redemptive ways, because at the core of my discipleship is the belief that every human being is an individual, unique soul of worth and promise, loved by Heavenly Parents, and deserving of all opportunities to overcome challenges and to reach her or his full potential through Jesus Christ's loving atonement. So please just imagine with me that we are all lying on the grass in my backyard, waiting and watching as two great celestial spheres gradually creep toward each other, culminating in a beautiful corona and wrapping us all in an inclusive and welcoming new light. This is my vision of how the gospel brings us together in love and hope. Is there any wider circle that we can draw around ourselves?

## NOTES

1. Neylan McBaine, *Women at Church: Magnifying LDS Women's Local Impact* (Draper, UT: Greg Kofford Books, 2014), 19.

2. Julie M. Smith, "As Sisters in Zion," in *A Book of Mormons: Latter-day Saints on a Modern-Day Zion*, edited by Emily W. Jensen and Tracy McKay-Lamb (Ashland, OR: White Cloud Press, 2015), 29–30.

3. Smith, "As Sisters in Zion," 31.

4. McBaine, *Women at Church,* 23.

5. This, then, becomes Christ's call, that "he inviteth them all to come unto him and partake of his goodness; and he denieth none that come unto him, black and white, bond and free, male and female; and he remembereth the heathen; and all are alike unto God, both Jew and Gentile" (2 Nephi 26:33).

6. Andrea G. Radke-Moss, "A Love Letter to Mormon Women on the Anniversary of the Relief Society, from a Mormon Historian and Feminist," *Juvenile Instructor*, March 17, 2015.

7. Edwin Markham, "Outwitted," in *The Shoes of Happiness and Other Poems* (Garden City and New York: Doubleday, Page, and Co., 1915), 1.

# When You Know the Truth

## ALICE BROBBEY

Courtesy of the author

Alice Brobbey was born on the warm, sunny Caribbean island of St. Maarten. She is a teacher by profession and enjoys reading, writing poetry, dancing, singing, and taking walks. She resides in Ghana, West Africa, with her husband and three daughters, one of whom is Alixa, whose essay also appears in this volume.

"There are two pilots outside who want some water," my little brother announced nonchalantly as he strolled into the house.

"What?" My sister and I looked at each other, confused. On the picturesque island of St. Maarten, that didn't seem possible, because we lived nowhere close to the airport. There was absolutely no reason for pilots to be in our area unless they had been in a plane crash, and then they would probably require more than water. We decided to humour our brother anyway. Standing at our gate were two young, white men looking like pilots in white shirts, navy-blue pants, and dark ties. They introduced themselves as missionaries from The Church of Jesus Christ of Latter-day Saints and said they had a message to share with us. We invited them into our home, and they taught us the gospel of Jesus Christ. After several weeks of teaching, inviting us to read certain scriptures and encouraging us to pray for our own confirmation, they invited us to church. Now, growing up on a Caribbean island, I was no stranger to religion. It was a part of my everyday life. In fact, by the time I met the missionaries at the age of thirteen, I had attended the Baptist church as a toddler, the Seventh-Day Adventist church as a preschooler and received my first holy communion in the Catholic church at the age of seven. Every Sunday afternoon my siblings and I attended a neighbourhood Sunday School, and on some evenings my sister and I attended an evangelical church in the hopes of saving our souls from the eternal damnation they always preached about. We accepted the missionaries' invitation.

I will never forget our first sacrament meeting. The white apartment we met in was small and pretty empty. We couldn't believe that this was the meetinghouse. There were no more than ten of us gathered, including the missionaries and four members of my family. The messages were shared in a soft tone, and they did not preach damnation. Instead, they taught love. The sacrament was administered with water and regular bread. The songs they sang were unfamiliar, the method of praying strange and they called each other brother and sister. As our little family walked out of the building and entered our car, we talked about what a weird experience it had been. The main thing that stood out, however, was the way we felt. Everyone was welcoming and friendly and the tone was filled with love instead of trying to invoke fear. Later, we would come to learn that what we had felt was the Spirit. All we knew then is that we had never felt that way before, and we wanted to feel it again.

We continued to attend church, and then one day the missionaries invited us to be baptized. While my father had enjoyed getting to know the missionaries, he was not interested in joining the Church. My mom had a testimony of what they were teaching, but she was not ready to commit. My brother was too young for baptism, but my sister and I chose to be baptized. We were very excited to share the great news with our friends and family. Big mistake! Everyone we talked to tried to dissuade us. They told us that the Church was a cult, or the anti-Christ, and that their pastors had warned them about it. Some of our friends told us that they could no longer be our friends if we went ahead with our decision to be baptized. We were surprised by their reactions but felt strongly that this was something we wanted to do. We knew it, we believed it, we felt it. The Spirit had testified of its truthfulness and we could not deny it. We became the first members of the Church to be baptized on our little island. The joy I felt on that day was so poignant, so real. It was a feeling I could never forget. As we sang "I Am a Child of God," the words became so real to me!

After our baptism, the persecution continued. People were always eager to tell us that our church practiced polygamy. They told us that our church was racist and didn't like Black people. They told us that the church was secretive and evil. I wondered about the stories of polygamy. I questioned the racist background of the Church, particularly when the missionaries at that time taught us that we had to marry within our own race because interracial relationships were not encouraged. Despite this, my sister and I pressed on. We gave talks. We taught lessons. We served in various callings. It was hard work and a lot of pressure. I missed having the life of a regular teenager. I missed going to a church where all I needed to do was show up on Sunday and be preached to. Eventually, I became less active. Then, at the tender age of twenty-one, I lost my mother. I questioned the Lord for taking away my mother, my world, my everything. There were days when I felt my world had ended, days I felt bitter, days I felt discouraged and all alone. It was too painful to go back to the Church. Instead, I attended other churches with my friends, hoping to feel comfort and peace. But as I listened to pastors and ministers speak, I would mentally correct their doctrine. It was evident that I could not join any other church. I knew that the time would come that I would have to return to the truth I knew. I could not deny it, and nothing else could compare.

In my mid-twenties, I moved to the Netherlands. I found the missionaries and invited them into my home. I resolved that this time I would not depart from the truth I had known and felt. During the coming years, I would see that resolve tested in many ways. I would find that life's greatest challenges, tests, hurts, and disappointments sometimes come from within the membership of the Church, from the very ones we call our brothers and sisters, from the very ones we are to love and care for. These experiences are hard to witness and hear about, but as I reflect on them, I am reminded that we are not members of the Church because we are perfect but because we are striving to be more like Christ. As the Savior says in Matthew 9:12, "They that be whole need not a physician, but they that are sick." We all need a physician. None of us is completely whole. The Lord uses us, "the weak things," to show forth his miracles, to strengthen us and to teach us (see 1 Corinthians 1:27). We are all a work in progress as we strive to overcome our own imperfections, interpretations, weaknesses, past experiences, and influences and become more like our Saviour. We must strive to choose the culture of Christ, the culture of love above that of anything else.

As a foreigner now living in Ghana, there are still challenging issues facing the Church that often result in members becoming less committed or leaving the Church. But I stand firm, and I hold to the truths I know. Taking on the culture of Christ allows me to see others through His eyes, to forgive rather than to hold a grudge, to encourage rather than put down and, most importantly, to love without conditions. I often remind myself that we are all trying our best, so let us be patient with ourselves and others. It is not an easy road we have chosen, but we know that it will be worthwhile in the end.

My experiences in the Caribbean, in Europe, and now in Africa remind me that while the Church is the Lord's, we cannot expect the people in the Church to be perfect. We are all influenced by the society in which we live. If we are not careful, society will influence our Church culture and the way we treat each other. Our challenges may be different, depending on how we are seen and where we find ourselves. At times we may see, hear, and experience things we don't like or don't expect in the Church. We may even question, "How could this possibly be the true church if . . . ?" Whatever it is, I try to remind myself that though none of us is perfect, we all have a place in God's kingdom. I remind myself of my own imperfections and that the Lord still uses me in spite of them. I remind myself of the miracles I have experienced, of the healing power of Christ's Atonement, of the pure joy I've felt repenting and getting back on the covenant path. I have experienced having my needs met after paying tithing. I have experienced the love and friendship of people of all colours, cultures, countries, social classes, and walks of life. I have felt God's love for all of His children. After everything I have been through, and continue to go through, I have found my own confirmation of the truth and cannot depart from it. It keeps me going each day as I remember that I am His child. He will continue to lead and guide me if I trust in Him and allow him to. I will forever be grateful for the curiosity of a six year old and the willingness of two young "pilots" to dedicate two years of their lives to preaching the gospel on a tiny island in the middle of the Caribbean Sea.

# DIVINITY IN MOTHERHOOD

Righteous women have changed the course of history and will continue to do so, and their influence will spread and grow exponentially throughout the eternities.

—*Julie B. Beck*

# In Story, the Branch Buds

## ROSALYNDE WELCH

Rosalynde Welch is an independent scholar of literature, philosophy, and theology of The Church of Jesus Christ of Latter-day Saints. She holds a PhD in early modern English literature from the University of California at San Diego. Her writing appears in Mormon studies–related journals and books, as well as in Latter-day Saint blogs and the *St. Louis Post-Dispatch*. She lives in St. Louis, Missouri, with her husband and four children.

Danica Nelson

We sit on the edge of the sea, my sisters and I, our eyes trained on a dozen small heads bobbing in the waves as a trio of babes surf the aunties' willing arms. Pelicans dive and clouds sail to the sun. We talk in the wandering way of beach conversations about everything and nothing, more to practice the old rhythms of being together than anything else. Sometimes the words catch a breeze off the gulf, and a story rises between us, a kite tethered by threads of memory. These stories, tugging at the sandy stakes of the past, are grounded in actual people and places, but they rise toward a second draft of our shared history. Their arcs trace our hopes for the future as much as the events of our lives. My sister tells a story about our mother's past to track our twining identities forward to the waterline where the children play; I tell a story about our childhood to launch urgent hopes for my daughter. Our stories, as layered as the coastal clouds, ply possible futures with usable pasts.

Here is a story my mother tells about me. *We were camping at Mammoth Lake, awaiting the firework display that would begin after dark. The little kids were getting restless, so I asked Rosalynde to join me in taking them for a walk. She was fourteen years old, my faithful helper with our seven children at the time. I thought I knew this daughter of mine; in fact, I was certain I was creating her to be a more perfect version of me. I felt a maternal glow as we strolled with our eyes on our little ones. Out of the blue, it seemed to me, she looked at me and blurted out, "So is this how it's supposed to be: you got a college education so you could stay at home and raise a bunch of girls whom you would get educated and send to college so they can stay at home and raise a bunch of kids? Is that the plan? I just don't get it!" It felt like someone had punched me in the stomach. But in an instant I realized that maybe, just maybe, there was more than one right way to be a daughter of God—maybe my choices were not the one and only true choices for all my daughters. It was a paradigm-shifting moment in my life, landing me in a life filled with more uncertainty, more researching and soul-searching, fewer pat answers and unexamined assumptions, but a whole lot more truth and growth and wonder.*

The dance of difference and likeness clasps every mother-daughter pair. Like most stories, this one is more about the teller than the told-about. Do you see how it works? My prickly adolescent questioning provides the narrative grist, but in the end it's my mother's sense of her own opened mind that emerges from the story. We raise our daughters in our own images—how can we do otherwise?—but with the grace of growing things, they crack those expectations wide like a shoot from a seed. It's a painful loss—a punch in the stomach, as my mother says—to confront the reality that our daughters' lives are not our doubles and our mothers' lives are not our maps. Perhaps it's a mother's gut-felt sense of her own aging, underscored daily by her children's surging physical growth, that provokes anxiety to draw her daughters close within the path: *she'll be there to carry on when I'm gone.* My mother tells this story to push beyond the anxiety, to make it true that trust and beauty may be found not only in the cleaving but also in the *branching* of the daughter's way, however well-loved and well-mapped her own. Trees have often communicated women's connection to the sacred; for some Latter-day Saints, as for other believers, the biblical tree of life can be seen to represent the wisdom of the divine feminine. And what is that wisdom? Lesson one: that every tree must branch before it buds. The branching of the tree expands its communion with the sun, and under its warm breath new leaves emerge to make visible the hidden potential of the air. My mother tells the story to make it possible for my sisters and me to branch away from the good wood of her own life choices and to give form to her faith that we will find our own places under the same loving heaven.

Stories have a way of turning to face each other. Here is a story I tell about my mother, about a story she told me about myself. *My mother, who graduated from a rural high school with few opportunities, drank deeply at BYU's wells of study and faith. Her intelligence attracted my father, and one morning my mother arrived in her mentor's office explaining that she was engaged and had no time for his upper division seminar. The professor told her that she shouldn't waste her potential by marrying in college; she should apply to a graduate program instead. Come back tomorrow, he said, if you're still determined to get married, and I'll sign off. But think hard about it. My mother wrestled with his words. She returned the next day. The year that she would have started a graduate program, she gave birth to me instead. You are my graduate degree, she told me. And I've never regretted the sacrifice for an instant. She told me this story after I finished my own PhD, married, and was now raising two babies. I'm so proud of you, she told me. You did what I couldn't. And your children will be blessed if you sacrifice to stay home with them. You're giving up worldly honor for the most important work in the world. You'll never regret it. She was right: I have no regret. "But here's the thing," I always say as I conclude the story. "It's never felt like sacrifice or obedience to me. It feels more like figuring out what work life has granted me in this hour's square of sunshine."*

Even as I tell it, I taste a slick of oil on that last line. But there must be a reason that I tell the story this way, with a bit of slippage at the end where I break from my mother's story. Perhaps I want to make it true that a daughter can branch from her mother's course without rejecting it or her. I want to make it true that my mother's sacrifice of education and career for family *was* meaningful and necessary and generous and blessed—for me especially, who, after all, was brought to life because of her choice. I want to affirm the truth of my mother's story about herself. And I want to affirm the goodness of the ideas and institutions that stand behind her story of sacrifice: the Church and its culture, the centrality of family bonds in human experience, the holiness of losing one's ego in service of others. I hold the same wish for my Church foremothers: to honor the sacrifices they made to live in polygamy and consecration, to recognize the goodness of the Church to which they gave all, to draw strength from the good wood of their lives.

I also want to make it true that the goodness of those ideas and institutions leafs out again for my generation and for my daughter's. Here is the wisdom of the tree: some branches must push away from the trunk to find the sun. My life doesn't follow my mother's life—my mothers' lives—in every particular, and my stories put notions of sacrifice and selflessness to a different work than do theirs. I shape my story around the work of discerning and submitting to the call of life, whereas my mother shapes hers around sacrificing ego for family; my story is about the care and keeping of each day's new creation, whereas hers is about trusting in the blessings of obedience. I've labored over these sentences, trying to make them honor both my mother's experience and my own, trying to give form to our differences without dismissal. I'm not yet satisfied with the shape. My story is always subject to revision; revision is inescapable, because I've written it into the always evolving structure of the story itself. Soon I'll find myself summoned into my daughter's stories, no longer the branch but the maternal trunk, receding into the intricate fractal branching that time works upon family generations to conjure eternity between repetition and difference. Will the sap flow, the sun shine, the twigs bud for them?

Here is a story I tell about my daughter. *When Elena was small, I couldn't wait to teach her to play the piano. I researched methods, I bought the books, and I sat beside her at the piano every day. At first she enjoyed it, but as "Twinkle Twinkle" became "Für Elise," her progress slowed. I could see the pleasure had gone out of the process for her, though she remained anxious to please me. But I doubled down. More practice, more intensity, more anxiety for her, more frustration for me, all driven by something inside me I couldn't quite name. There was vicarious vanity, yes, but why did I always picture her playing in the comically parochial context of our church meetings—accompanying hymns in Young Women, performing in sacrament meeting? Growing up, I had played in those settings weekly, and my sense of belonging at church centered on the piano. I found there a necessary role, a respected responsibility that contributed visibly to the community and involved me in collaborative effort that mattered to the whole. At the piano, I felt significant to my faith community in a way that I rarely did elsewhere. And I wanted that for my daughter. The urgency of my hopes for Elena's progress on the piano measured the urgency of my hopes for her sense of belonging and connection to the church I loved.*

Some stories we tell simply for the life they breathe. *My great-great-grandmother Maude Mary Taylor grew up in Colonia Juárez, Mexico, where her people had gone to practice their religion as they chose. Maude had long red hair that hung in braided pigtails down her back. She was known as the fastest runner in the village, swifter than any of the boys. When she ran, the red braids flew in the wind she created with her own speed.*

This story needs no analysis. Its work is as intuitive and deft as bird's flight. It stitches the past to the future in a single image of freedom and joy. It performs the hopes of every mother, the longings of every daughter. Its roots go deep and its branches reach high, ever green. It shows us how, in the telling of our stories, we act on the world—not unilaterally but in concert with the intelligent elements and agents with which we share it. We tell our stories, as mundane as piano scales or as sublime as fluttering red braids, in an ongoing work of creation that draws us to the divine.

# The Women Unwritten

## ASHLEY MAE HOILAND

Ashley Mae (Ashmae) Hoiland received a BFA in painting and an MFA in creative writing from Brigham Young University, Provo, Utah. She is the author of *100 Birds Taught Me to Fly* and the illustrator of *Mother's Milk: Poems Searching for Heavenly Mother*. A writer at the By Common Consent blog, she lives in Santa Cruz, California, with her three children and husband.

Paige Smith

There is a rocking chair in the corner of my children's room. Most nights before they go to bed, I read them library books, and we end with a chapter of the Book of Mormon. In these past months as I've read with my children, I've started doing something simple that has changed my reading. In the places where it says, "My sons," I simply add, "and daughters." In places where it says "Brothers," I also add "Sisters." I include female pronouns wherever appropriate. As I add in these phrases, maybe because it makes me feel a little sneaky, I sometimes look up at Remy and Thea to see if they notice, but no, of course they don't. To them, their own worlds are filled with examples of strong men and women, so why would the scriptures be any different? And it's true, why would the experiences depicted in the scriptures be any different?

In my own life, as I've gotten older, the work of trying to be Christlike has come down to two simple ideas: learning to look and find where people need to be seen and then listening to them. I understood that the women who needed to be seen and listened to are the women I do not see at all, including those in scripture—the women I refer to as "sisters, daughters, wives, widows, friends." In short, *she* and *her*. These perceived *shes* and *hers* that are not written about in the Book of Mormon have become increasingly notable to me because in so many ways, my contemporary experience mirrors theirs.

As I read the scriptures with the unmentioned women who were certainly there but not written about, in my mind the Book of Mormon becomes abuzz with the underpinnings of female lives and voices. I see them forming circles. I see them working. I see them as leaders in their communities, even if subversively for the time. I see them helping to raise one another's children. I see them as strong, and I see them as wanting to be spoken of in our present day.

Most recently I've been reading in Mosiah with my kids. One scene I have been familiar with my whole life but have never fully imagined is the part where King Benjamin is speaking from a tower to the people. The narrator mentions that women and children are present as the scene is set up, but then the women move into the background of the text, and King Benjamin addresses "brethren" throughout his speech. What has struck me in recent reading is that when I really try to imagine this scenario, I first see a small scattering of women here and there. But the more I try to picture the scene, the more clearly I see that they are not only a handful of women but also a landscape of vibrant and diverse women. They are busy doing work. They are ready to listen. They are smart and capable. They are wrangling children and feeding them proverbial cheerios. They are helping each other. They are cleaning the tent. They are making plans. They are laughing. They are notable to me because I see my own life playing out in that landscape, and I love them, these long-ago sisters who also believed in Christ, who were trying to do good.

As I delve further into Book of Mormon stories, I start to hear a hum of women, first quiet, almost indiscernible, but the hum of their work and lives grows louder and more abundant in my mind until it is not just women being present and active in the scene before King Benjamin but throughout the whole Book of Mormon. I see these women, women of all types—married, unmarried, old, young, of many different colors and economic classes—and they are not stagnant characters.

I don't have to imagine very hard to see them in my mind. I feel like my own lived experience has provided enough threads to weave a thousand rich tapestries. Women are, in various ways, undoubtedly an integral part of every major event, but it's also likely that they will not be the ones who get to have their story spotlighted. These stories are often so regular, so innocuous, so quotidian, so part of the background that we fail to tell these stories because we fail to see the ways in which the diverse stories of women are the foundations of nations.

In a women's conference nearly two decades ago, Sheri Dew said something that resonates with me as I grapple with my own notions of being notable in today's world: "My message to you today, my dear sisters, whom I love, is the same: There is nothing more vital to our success and our happiness here than learning to hear the voice of the Spirit. It is the Spirit who reveals to us our identity—which isn't just who we are but who we have always been. And that when we know, our lives take on a sense of purpose so stunning that we can never be the same again."[1]

In these past months as I've read the Book of Mormon, I've seen a heritage of sisterhood that does help me to know not just who I am now but, in a sense, where I come from. I see in my mind's eye this vast movement of women and in them I see part of my own identity. I am bolstered by the image of them. These imagined women who are not named, not even hinted at in word, are notable to me in part because I have to believe that in all my own plainness in this world, I am still notable to my Heavenly Parents.

I know there are hundreds of ways to be a woman in the world today, but I'll speak to my own experience. Living here in Palo Alto, California, I have come to truly love the quiet but strong voices of women who are not always the obvious heroes of the story, the voices that can seem invisible to the world but have done the work of showing me what it is to be loved and cared for in godly ways. Many of the women who have changed and shaped my life are not the "notable" women; in fact, it's likely that no one will write and tell their story. It's likely that our conversations, revelations, and intellect will remain buried in the sand and hanging on the play structures of the courtyards where we spent so many hours while our children played. When we first came to Stanford for graduate school, I was resistant to "mom conversations." I had a desire to be an intellectual or at least come off that way. It didn't take me long, though, to see that the two are not mutually exclusive.

There will be almost no record of the many incredible women I've known in my time here. It's likely that the husbands of many of them will leave behind written records of dissertations, names on certificates and awards and in academic journals. But for many of the women I know, the written and spoken record in the halls of academic and worldly success simply will not be there. The women who feel that the world is moving swiftly past them and that they cannot make their voice loud enough to be heard, or maybe they feel that they don't even have something important enough to say loudly in the first place, have become the most notable women in the world to me. They are the stories of the women who have moved me, who have helped raise my children and formed circles around me in dark and tired hours, who have celebrated me as I've done for them. The women, who likely don't feel notable, have time and again done the work of seeing me when I needed to be seen and listened to me when I thought no one would care.

I picture women also in relation to Christ. I think of the women in the New Testament, some of whom are named but many of whom are not. In their proximity to Christ, their willingness to believe that they might be healed, forgiven, listened to, or able to speak, was magnified. The woman with an issue of blood was healed, the woman taken in adultery was forgiven, the woman at the well was listened to, and the widow with her two mites was able to speak.

I wonder then what I am doing in my own life to give voice to the marginalized groups around me. I wonder how I can be Christlike in doing the work that others sometimes cannot do for themselves. In what ways am I seeing those who need to be seen and listening to them when they are found? Am I offering my platform to those who don't normally get to speak? I am continually moved when I read the scriptures at the ability and insistence that Christ had for making what was typically not notable, notable.

We have a great work to do to ensure that we do not move forward as a Church just having to imagine what the voices of the marginalized might be. We can make room to hear diverse voices from the single people, people of color, the people with and without degrees, the people in poverty, the divorced, the women who work outside the home and the women who work inside the home, the physically or mentally sick, the abused, and the displaced.

Again and again Jesus offers dignity to people in situations where the law offers only judgment. What are we doing to give space and voice to the people who typically do not hold power? How do we make notable what could be deemed unnotable? How do we make sure our modern scripture forms circles around women so we do not leave them out of entire books? How do we mirror Christ's compassion toward all people? "Have ye any that are sick among you? Bring them hither. Have ye any that are lame, or blind, or halt, or maimed, or leprous, or that are withered, or that are deaf, or that are afflicted in any manner? Bring them hither and I will heal them, for I have compassion upon you; my bowels are filled with mercy" (3 Nephi 17:7).

For me, I think the answer will always be found in what Christ repeatedly taught. Simply look, and then listen. I am changed when I think of the woman with an issue of blood, the way she was listened to, when to herself she said, "If I may but touch his garment, I shall be whole" (Matthew 9:21). Christ likely was listening and made her notable within a crowd when she had probably been considered anything but notable.

Finally, maybe we can learn also to be okay with not being notable all the time. In reading about Christ's interactions with the people in 3 Nephi, no names are mentioned, only a crowd of men, women, and children. Are we not also simply a participant in that crowd? When I read that passage, I imagine a group of regular people, both men and women, both marginalized and not. I see them also forming circles, bolstering one another, notable to no one except to Christ, who seeks them out one by one and blesses them and blesses them and blesses them.

NOTE

1. Sheri L. Dew, "Knowing Who You Are—and Who You Have Always Been," in *Ye Shall Bear Record of Me: Talks from the 2001 BYU Women's Conference* (Salt Lake City: Bookcraft, 2002), 278, https://womensconference.byu.edu/sites/womensconference.ce.byu.edu/files/dew _sheri_2.pdf.

# Someday My Children Will Come

## MARIE-FRANÇOISE EUVRARD

Marie-Françoise Euvrard was born in Paris, France, and joined The Church of Jesus Christ of Latter-day Saints in 1960. She is the mother of two wonderful boys whom she and her husband adopted from Nepal. Professionally, she is a piano teacher and translates hymns and songs for the Church. She and her husband, Christian, serve as directors of the visitors' center adjacent to the temple in Rome, Italy.

Amrit Euvrard

For decades, I dreamed of being and doing so many different things. Along those years, what I prayed the Lord to grant me often wasn't given, and my desires slowly changed. Looking back over my life, I now see that He broadened my horizons more than I could ever have imagined and offered me experiences that gave me more joy than I had ever expected.

I was born right in the middle of the city of Paris, the only child of parents who were much older than the parents of any of my friends. Growing up, I attended girls' schools and had only female teachers. Even after my parents and I joined The Church of Jesus Christ of Latter-day Saints when I was eight years old, I had little interaction with boys my age because there was no one my age in our Paris Branch. In fact, the closest teens or young adults in the branch were five or more years older than I, and I was too shy to associate with those so much older. So with my mother serving as Primary president, I continued attending Primary to avoid activities with older kids. I taught the ten- and eleven-year-old boys and served as Primary secretary. Even though my mother taught me how to be a good mother to my dolls, I had few opportunities to be reassured that a woman's life in the Church could be rich and rewarding.

At age twenty, I was called to serve as a coleader in our area's M-Men and Gleaner program, the predecessor of today's Young Adult program in the Church. The assignment required me to serve alongside a young man called as the other coleader. Wonder of wonders, I began falling in love with him and decided to serve a mission at the same time he did. What a surprise it was to learn that we had been called to serve in the very same mission. The Lord had humorous ways to prepare me for what He had in store for me.

One year after our missions, Christian and I were married for time and eternity. As newlyweds, we identified so many wonderful projects we planned to accomplish together, including the blessing we both desired most: starting our family. Although nothing happened quite the way we had imagined, our married life was remarkable and fulfilling: we moved nine times between France and Italy, established ourselves in careers that opened many doors for us to serve the broader Church, and learned leadership, compassion, and hope from interactions with people and cultures from around the world.

But our dream for children continued to evade us. This dream took more time—much more time. Our newlywed plans never counted on years of medical treatments; painful Relief Society lessons that focused on educating our children; or what felt like thousands of people constantly asking, "How many children do you have?"; our parents' concerned and impatient question, "What is happening?"; and our own fervent and often short-tempered prayers that were always full of tears.

Those years followed a long and winding path, but I learned so much along the way. From prayer I learned patience and the real power of the Comforter. Many nights I cried to the Lord with tears on my pillow, feeling depressed and hopeless. Every morning I woke up with hope and new happy projects for the day: The Holy Ghost had used His healing power during my sleep. I must say also that quite often on Sunday I went to church with an angry and sometimes rebellious heart. It seemed to me that each sacrament meeting talk or each lesson showed only one model to obtain eternal life: be married in the temple and produce a sweet family with as many children as you can imagine. I called it the "Church Playmobile Family" principle.

However, I also learned from the scriptures during those years that such a model is not described in them. The scriptures do talk about men of God who struggled to find a good wife and about good women who were childless for many years. The scriptures describe their humiliation and despair as they held on with faith and obedience. In some of these stories, childless women even became mothers of prophets! Church leaders in general conference also comforted me with the reality of a "non-Playmobile happiness." The Relief Society curriculum changed from focusing on motherhood and homemaker training to living the gospel. Women without children, such as Ardeth Kapp and Sheri Dew, were called to high Church responsibilities and proved to me that the Lord was no respecter of persons. He loves His daughters who do not bear children just as He loves those daughters who do.

Most of all, the Lord provided me wonderful alternatives to motherhood through service in His Church. I served many times in Primary, where I had the opportunity to teach little ones, have fun with them, and feel their love. I served in Young Women, taught seminary, and was able to help teenagers find their way in the gospel and experience happiness in difficult times. And what an amazing opportunity to accompany my husband to Italy, where I served with my husband when he was called as mission president. I was mission mother, as they called me, to 386 elders and sisters who were only ten years younger than I!

The answer didn't come for twenty years. Twenty years. After we have been married for twenty years, the solution came softly into my mind and heart. Adoption.

In 1990, with the French Adoption Agreement and a convocation letter from the Kathmandu Orphanage Organization in my suitcase, I embarked for Nepal to bring our first child home. Yes, our kids were born under the "roof of the world," at the feet of the Himalayan Mountains! I thought I would return with our son in ten days, but it turned out to be five weeks. Every day, I cried at the Nepalese Home Ministry when I heard repeatedly that I couldn't return to France with my son. Again, I relied on fervent prayers, daily loving encouragements by phone from my husband, a special fast by the members of our stake, and the providential help of an American family I met in the Kathmandu Branch. They took me into their home and nurtured me physically and spiritually. Eventually, I was able to take a child by the hand and hear him call me the sweetest name: "maman." His out-standing older brother joined our family only two years later, after many other steps and emotional ups and downs between disappointments, hope, and waiting.

We now have a wonderful family with joys and challenges such as those any other family knows. The Lord, in His love, spared me the pain of childbirth. I am so thankful for that. But I think—somewhere and somehow—I actually survived twenty years of pregnancy and five weeks and two years of delivery! I have tasted the tender mercies of the Lord. My Savior comforted and instructed me in my expectations. He gently took me by the hand to lead me where He knew I would find more wisdom and happiness than in the path I envisioned.

Today, I rejoice to be a woman, a wife, a mother, and a grand-mother. But above all, I rejoice that I am a daughter of God, Who knows me.

# CAREER AND FAMILY

Let us have educated, refined, common-sense mothers, and the home, society, the nation, and the world will reap the benefits.

—*Mattie Horne Tingey*

# "Why Not Both?"
# A Lesson in Choosing More

## JARICA WATTS

Jarica Linn Watts is an assistant professor of English at Brigham Young University, Provo, Utah. She specializes in British literature from the early twentieth century, particularly the short fiction of World War I. Fashion (Italian shoes), fitness (marathon running), photography (Canon), and her two children (a girl and a boy) bring her round to herself.

Several years ago, I found myself thirty weeks pregnant and unexpectedly in labor, experiencing contractions in a poorly lit labor and delivery suite with five suddenly awkward English professors by my side. It was two years before I graduated with a PhD in British literature, a few more before I landed a professorship at Brigham Young University, and more still before I'd become the mother of two.

It was January 25, 2008—author Virginia Woolf's birthday, a footnote that was not lost on me even then—and I had been studying for my PhD qualifying exam for well over a year. Aside from graduation, this is *the* moment in a doctoral student's life: a four-hour oral defense that's meant to serve as a threshold between coursework and dissertation. It was to be my own landing on the moon. A personal toppling of the Berlin Wall. An initiation that would signal the beginning of the end of my formal education. We were knee-deep in a winter that showed no signs of relenting. The economy would soon collapse, within a few months all of academia would be in a hiring freeze, and a career in the humanities felt like a fool's errand.

My exam had been scheduled for a year. My water broke at two in the morning. Exam day. Besides shock, my strongest impression was a particular, crippling sort of frustration. I left home with nothing but a business suit, my small briefcase stuffed with novels and notes sitting uncomfortably atop my pregnant belly as we drove the thirty miles to the hospital. I did my best to navigate the bags and the anxiety and the fluid that was flowing so freely from my body.

"I'll be back," I assured the nurse at my university's hospital. "I have to take a test on campus for a few hours, and then I'll be back," I insisted. In disbelief, she shook her head: "I'm sorry, but you're not leaving here without a baby." My hands began to shake, my body seethed, and as I became increasingly upset, she grew calmer in direct proportion. "But you don't understand," I pleaded. "I'll be right back."

To provide some context, all this was happening two months earlier than I had anticipated my baby's arrival. I was entirely preoccupied by the year's worth of studying I had done—a year's worth of studying that had suddenly crescendoed at the exact moment my daughter was trying to make her entrance into the world. As the clock ticked from the middle of the night into the very early morning, my doctor entered the room. I had a choice to make: I could either take or cancel the exam, but I could not leave the hospital. If I chose to take the exam, my committee would have to come to me. All of this, of course, was predicated on the fact that I.WAS.HAVING.A.BABY! Everything felt in-between, myself most of all.

As night sank to day, I called the chair of my committee. I could hear the annoyance in his voice as I explained the situation; he suggested, predictably, that we reschedule the exam for later in the semester. My family slowly arrived, and each person had an opinion: "Baby—first and always," chimed my husband; "Listen to your body," whispered my mom; "It's up to you," my dad declared. Consensus fell on the side of postponing; I did, after all, have a baby on the way—at this point it was an extremely high-risk pregnancy—and the social worker assigned to help me navigate our daughter's early arrival insisted that I needed my strength for whatever the next hours or days may bring. "I understand your position," my doctor who holds both an MD and a PhD whispered, "I really do. *But still* . . . ," she said, letting the words trail off. It was a few hours full of so many *What ifs*, shifting sand in an ocean of uncertainty. The day before, I knew where my story was going, and with one little trickle—or was it a gush?—the ground shifted beneath my swollen feet.

But a small tug of the gut reminded me of something I had once heard: Courage requires first a decision and then a leap. And so, the question I kept asking—and the question I keep asking—is *why not both? Why can't I do both?* In a moment of rare grit, I determined that if my committee would come, I would take the exam. I was eventually scheduled for an ultrasound, but the procedure was interrupted by my mother: "They're on their way," she chuckled, a quiet laugh born of nerves. My committee was coming to me, a gesture that, even now, feels exceptionally generous. There was an odd and constant shuffle of people in the hospital that day, but I remain most aware of and grateful for the woman from central laundry who brought me a fresh pair of scrubs.

I was breathless and a little unkempt when I was wheeled back into my room, but, dressed in the hospital's best pair of blue, borrowed scrubs, I felt utterly prepared for what might come. That's when I saw my committee, already seated around my inclined hospital bed, ready to pounce. I was overwhelmed with a tidal wave of *Oh, dear* and began to stutter, "I'm good. I'm good to go now. I'm ready." They were English professors—without doubt, they had to be thinking of *Hamlet,* act 3, scene 2: "The lady doth protest too much."

We covered a lot of ground, quickly. They watched as I squirmed and listened as I mumbled. Four hours later, my committee walked out of the room and down the hall to deliberate on whether I had passed the exam. "Pass her!" the medical residents outside my door all cheered, startling me with their presence. My doctor had been monitoring my progress and came to tell me that she would not be able to stave off my labor any longer. I had to prepare for emergency surgery. As I was wheeled into the operating room, my committee emerged. Against all odds, I had passed! I was having a baby! And that's how it came to be that, within the very same hour, I became a PhD candidate and a first-time mother—a collision that has left me perpetually wondering whether the chicken or the egg came first.

As women in the gospel, we are frequently asked to make hard choices. And on that cold January morning, I was in a circumstance where I had to choose. The question I asked that day—*why not both? Why can't I do both?*—has been the guiding metaphor in my life, as I've attempted to straddle the often conflicting, always rewarding, roles of professor and mother. When the days get long and the obligations mount, I think back to the long line of women before me who were also asked to make difficult choices.

I turn to the scriptures, and I think of Eve and wonder what she thought when confronted with a paradox of obedience: one decision over the other—both commandments. Would it be fruit or family? Indeed, she chose both. The Book of Mormon tells us of Sariah: she could give up on Laman and Lemuel, or she could continue to love and lead all of her children. She chose to love all her children perfectly, both the righteous and unrighteous—Laman and Lemuel, Nephi and Sam, and her many daughters in between (1 Nephi 1:1; 5:8; 18:17–18). We memorialize the mothers of the stripling warriors: They could dig up their weapons and defend their families, or they could honor their covenant never to fight again. Like Eve, they were up against paradox, and again like Eve, they chose both: to fight without weapons and, thereby, keep their promise (Alma 23: 6–7, 16–17; 24;12–27; 53:10–21; 56: 44–48, 55–56). For each of these women, the answer was repeatedly, again and again, not *either-or* but *both-and*.

Such scriptural accounts confirm that, as women of faith, we are frequently asked to find a way, to maximize our potential in the face of the seemingly impossible. But I live with the certitude and conviction that our Savior walks with us, and if we rely on him, he will not abandon us. Paul delivers a beautiful sermon in Philippians 4:12–13 that seems rife with conflicting notions: "Every where and in all things I am instructed both to be full and to be hungry, both to abound and to suffer need." I read Paul's words as a declaration to maximize our potential: to be *full* (to be grateful, content, satisfied) and to be *hungry* (to be driven, ambitious, a seeker); both to *abound* (to flourish, succeed, and accomplish one's goals) and to *suffer need* (to know that we cannot do it alone). Paul ends verse 13 with the declaration "I can do all things through Christ which strengtheneth me," that mirrors the Savior's own words in John 14:18: "I will not leave you comfortless."

I once would have told you that my personal brand of success would mean the ability to hold a career in one hand and a family in the other—to balance those seemingly opposing forces. But now, ask me how I manage my days, and I will tell you stories of messiness and chaos, of conflicting schedules and contrasting demands, of having too many obligations and too little time. I will tell you how balance is part of the story but how learning to embrace the imbalance—how to expect *and accept* the unexpected—is far more important. I will tell you that priorities ebb and flow and that embracing the imbalance means adopting a system of triage to assess degrees of urgency—all while knowing that resources are limited and the demand will always outweigh the supply. It's childbirth and qualifying exam at once.

As Latter-day Saint women, we will continue to be asked to make hard choices. But why are we inclined to limit the answer to *this* or *that*, black or white, one path over the other? It wasn't until I was forced to find a different avenue by which to achieve my goals that I realized I *could* choose both. At that moment, my world opened up. But why did it take such a dramatic event to expand my awareness? Why wasn't the *both-and* option in my mind long before my water broke? The scriptures, after all, give us wonderful examples of faithful women who wrestle and struggle and work their way around one commandment in order to fulfill another. *Why not both?* they ask time and again. *Why not more?*

I've come to believe that, more often than we're comfortable admitting, the answer is "all of the above," a frenzy of options rushing in together and somersaulting over each other. We must be alert enough to look for more and unrelenting in our pursuit of better and richer and fuller experiences. With the Lord's help, and with his confirmation, we *can* choose both: as women, we can maximize our potential, we can do *all things* as Paul decrees—in whatever capacity that looks like for each individual sister.

My workspace may never be free of tiny fingerprints and colorful scribbles, my home may never be devoid of stacks of papers needing to be graded. But I'm content with the chaos, just as I'm content with the calm. If the clash of childbirth and qualifying exam was in the service of that imbalance, okay then. Choosing both it is. Indeed, that January morning—now my daughter's birthday, a footnote that is not lost on me—became a valuable lesson in listening to that voice that wants more. And that's the best, most sincere truth I can offer.

# Mostly Messy
## Love Is Spoken

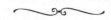

## MELISSA WEI-TSING INOUYE

Melissa Wei-Tsing Inouye was born and raised in Costa Mesa, California. A love of Chinese language and literature led her into PhD studies in East Asian languages and civilizations at Harvard University, Cambridge, Massachusetts. She is a senior lecturer in Asian Studies at the University of Auckland, Auckland, New Zealand, where she lives with her husband and four children.

YEARS: Where I've been

1979: My mother gives birth to me. She is twenty-one. She and my father look super happy in their hospital gowns. Nevertheless, in my father's phone call home, his voice is disappointed. "Mom," he says, "it's a girl." From here on, he doesn't let me wear things that are pink or girly.

1991: I turn twelve and enter Young Women. In an evening activity we hold roses and sing, "I am a princess." I have always taken a dim view of princesses. However, the Young Women leaders are kind. Their friendship makes a deep impression.

1997: Deciding where to go to college, I wonder aloud, "Does it really matter? I want to have kids, so maybe I'll never have a career anyway." "I think you can do both," my dad says. It sounds too good to be true; I was almost afraid to ask. Now I am almost afraid to hear. But it makes me happy.

2001: Standing at the pulpit of the Tainan Third Ward at the end of my mission, I recognize every upturned face and know something about the neighborhood, family relations, and work of each person. Beholding them, I love them (Mark 10:21). I feel, for just a moment, that I can comprehend the mind and heart of God.

2003: I am planning to marry my fiancé, Joseph, in the Salt Lake Temple. As an ordinance worker in the Boston Massachusetts Temple, I love the temple and know its sacred liturgies by heart. However, thinking ahead to the more patriarchal elements of the sealing ceremony I will encounter as a bride gives me pause. I mull it over for a long time. Eventually, this is what I think: The core of my marriage in the temple depends on the raw materials (me and my loved one) and the unspoken promises we make to each other, just by turning up, in God's presence. It's perhaps the sixth-happiest day of my life, but it is the best and most consequential decision I have ever made.

2004: After spending a year at Brigham Young University so Joseph could graduate, we move to Boston for my PhD. Joseph gets a job as a math teacher at a charter school. I'm still not sure what I'm going to do with my degree. Can one balance work and family? One day, I wonder about this aloud to one of my professors, an elderly and famous historian of China who has known me since I was an undergraduate. He says, matter-of-factly, "You're going to have to figure out how to be a working mom. You'll have kids and be a scholar. You'll be great." From then on, I just assume that is how it's going to be.

2006, 2008, 2010, 2012: I greet my four children. They are wailing and covered in goo. Each time I am surprised to see how different they look from what I expected. They guzzle greedily from my breasts. I hold them fiercely and smell their baby breath. Their eyes are clear and bright. My mother always said, "Babies' eyes are shiny because they've never told a lie." I jiggle them softly to sleep. Jiggle, jiggle, jiggle.

2007: I teach a class at Cal State LA. It's an evening class, and the classroom is haunted by a ghost who sings Chinese pop renditions of Song dynasty poetry. The commute is an hour each way, and the class is two hours long. When I return home, my breasts are always dripping with milk, and the baby and I are happy to reunite.

2008: My mother passes away after nearly two years with cancer. On that morning, I discover that I absolutely believe in life after death. My second son is six months old. We have pictures of him at the graveside, beaming with round cheeks and shiny eyes.

2009–2010: We go to China for my research on the True Jesus Church, a religious movement with a very familiar founding story. A guy prays, sees Jesus, and establishes the one true church—but in Beijing,

China, 1917. The members of the True Jesus Church are friendly and devout. They welcome me to church and ask whether I have ever wondered why there are so many different Christian denominations in the world and which is true.

2011: Harvard University sends my PhD diploma in the mail. We are about to go to Hong Kong for Joseph's corporate lawyer job. When we get to Hong Kong, the sidewalks are narrow and crowded. It is hot and sweaty. The mosquitos are tricky.

2014: We love living in Hong Kong, but Joseph hates his job. If he gets home early, he gets home at 10:30 p.m. "Normal" is midnight. We refer to the office as "Papa's house." Every night I cook dinner and pack it into containers. We board a downtown bus and have family dinner in the food court below the office. Eventually we decide we need to prioritize being together as a family. I apply for academic jobs and take a position at the University of Auckland. Joseph stays home with the kids for about a year and a half until we get settled. He hikes and grows food in the garden.

2017: I am diagnosed with colon cancer. I have surgery and then chemotherapy, which gives me chills. My aunt sends me thick knitted socks and a down jacket. My father sends us money to install a wood-burning firebox in the living room. Joseph lights a fire every morning. The university gives me medical leave with full pay. All day, I sit on my bed or at the kitchen table and type at my computer. I am extremely productive. Being cancerous is not fun, but it's not all horrible. There's still space to go on living.

A WEEK: Where I am

Tuesday: I teach three tutorials for History 222/322 (Imperial China) and take the kids to piano, cello, and capoeira (an Afro-Brazilian martial art). Everything falls apart when they get to capoeira, held in a classroom at the University of Auckland. They fiddle with the classroom computer. They hide underneath the tables. They slump about and display a rotten attitude. In disgust I pull them out of class early. In a withering tone, I tell them that they were unacceptably rude and I am very disappointed. We drive home in stony silence. Tears of frustration spring to my eyes.

Wednesday: I give a lecture on women in the Ming and Qing dynasties for History 222/322. I take the younger kids to Chinese class and my oldest kid to running club. In the car, he asks how we know we are really who we think we are and all sorts of other existential questions. At home, the kids get out their Chinese books and do their homework, all on their own. I am kind of shocked.

Thursday: I get up before dawn and board a flight to Boise, Idaho, via Los Angeles. It is a lot of flying.

Friday: I give a paper on Latter-day Saint refugees and missionaries in Hong Kong at the Mormon History Association meeting. I argue that while The Church of Jesus Christ of Latter-day Saint is formally tightly controlled through a vertical, centralized, American hierarchy, the horizontally oriented Church at the grassroots has significant cultural gravity. I observe that the Latter-day Saint tradition simultaneously inspires centralization and consolidation on the one hand, and expansion and diversification on the other.

Saturday: Some Latter-day Saint women friends come to my hotel room after the conference. I have asked them to pray for me. They encircle me and speak aloud in turn as moved by the Spirit. It is one of the most beautiful and fortifying spiritual experiences of my life. Throughout this long prayer, tears flow freely and I am continually snarfing boogies back into my head. If your sisters ever minister to you in this way, make sure you are prepared with a wad of tissues.

Sunday: During a layover in Los Angeles, I go to church with my father and grandmother. As we sing the sacrament hymn, I feel that my mother is also present. This makes sense.

Monday: I brainstorm ideas for a lesson on Black Latter-day Saint pioneers to teach to Primary kids in sharing time. These stories are important for three reasons. One, they show how in our Church's earliest days, the Prophet Joseph Smith had a vision of Zion in which all were alike unto God. Two, they testify that racist attitudes and policies toward Black Latter-day Saints in the past and lingering into the present day are sins for which we must all seek to make amends. Three, telling these difficult stories strengthens our pioneer ethos. As a people, Latter-day Saints are willing to work hard and travel to new places. We can draw on this ethos to build Zion in the twenty-first century, with all the bewildering and complex problems of our global society.

Tuesday: I return to Auckland in time to take the kids to capoeira. We do cartwheels and headstands and maculelê, a mock-machete-fighting dance in which we whack sticks together with a satisfying smack. I am full of the joy of existence, of being in my body, of moving and stretching and connecting. My seven-year-old daughter does a headstand and spins around in a circle on her head. We get into the car to drive home, laughing and chatting. Then the kids start to bicker in mean-spirited tones about whether or not Poseidon would beat Jesus in a fight. From the front seat, I shout them down. Aaarrrgh . . .

SUNDAY: Where we're going

I am teaching a Primary class a lesson on the book of Judges. The lesson material is interesting but also problematic. For instance, the story of Samson includes a passage in which Samson kills thirty people and steals their clothes so he can pay off a bet. This is not really the kind of behavior we are trying to encourage in our children. The book of Judges also includes the story of Deborah, who was cool because she was a judge and a prophetess. Her story is kind of messy too. Deborah judges Israel and helps Barak in a battle against Sisera's chariots of iron. Eventually when the defeated Sisera seeks refuge in the woman Jael's tent, Jael hammers a tent spike through Sisera's head. The following chapter is all about Deborah and Barak singing a song about how they killed Sisera with God's help. It would either be the best or the worst Primary-song-with-actions ever. The scriptures are wild and real. Prophets and prophetesses roam freely through a wilderness simultaneously illuminated and fried by the power of God. Sometimes we wish we could stick to only the tidy stories, but one can't stay in the visitors' center forever.

In the final hour, I am teaching sharing time and singing time. Sharing time is a lesson on the priesthood. An eight-year-old girl asks, "Why don't girls have the priesthood?" "That is a great question," I say. "Actually, everyone who acts in the name of God, when called by God to do a job, acts through the authority of the priesthood."[1]

There is kind of an expectant silence. Clearly the kids have observed that in our Church culture, priesthood is associated with maleness exclusively. I say, "So, 'Why don't women use the Aaronic or the Melchizedek Priesthood to do certain jobs at church like bless the sacrament or lead the ward?' I don't know a good answer for that. I do know that how we understand priesthood changes over time. For instance, in the Bible, for a long time only male descendants of an Israelite man named Levi held the priesthood. In our Church history, for a long time only some of the men in the world could hold the priesthood. Priesthood is power that God gives to humankind, but we don't understand everything because we aren't God. We can do our best with the knowledge and authority we have now."

For singing time, I teach the kids "Love Is Spoken Here." As a child I loved this song for its beautiful melody and harmony. In recent years I have liked it less because not everyone in our ward has a mother and father at home or parents who are Church members. I don't want to make kids feel as if they can't have love in their family if their family doesn't fit a prescribed mold. So today, instead of "mother" and "father," I ask them to name important people in their life who pray, who lead the way, who teach. We sing the song multiple times, using these people. Thus we have "I see my Nana kneeling with our family each day" and "With aunties and uncles leading the way."

I feel my Savior's love. Mine is a life in which every hour is blessed by the strength of priesthood power—through my sisters, my brothers, and my sacred covenants with God. I will seek to draw near to my Mother and Father in Heaven, to grow into the measure of what it means to be their child. Their faces and their strength are all around me. Love is spoken here, and I am thankful.

NOTE

1. Dallin H. Oaks, "The Keys and Authority of the Priesthood," *Ensign*, May 2014.

# Your Big Life

## NEYLAN MCBAINE

Neylan is cofounder and CEO of Better Days 2020 and founder of the Mormon Women Project, a nonprofit organization dedicated to mobilizing Latter-day Saint women by telling their stories and exploring opportunities for increasing their voice within the Church institution. The author of *Women at Church* and the mother of three daughters, Neylan lives in Salt Lake City, Utah.

My dear daughter,

You want a big life. On the way home from school, in the car, your face lights up when you talk about the newest self-driving car experiments you've read about in *National Geographic* that day or the advanced prosthetic limbs you saw demonstrated online. You've investigated programs at universities that would help you be a part of pioneering scientific teams. Or the ambassador to the United Nations. You'll take either. Already, as a teenager, you long to be part of a world beyond our suburban Salt Lake City home. Perhaps it is because you were born in San Francisco and attended school as a child in Boston and New York. You trail clouds of glory from a childhood in all these cities of visionaries and strivers.

Sometimes you get frustrated by the opinions you hear at school and at church in Young Women, opinions you feel devalue your dreams for yourself and that big life you long for. At school, some kids wonder aloud why Latter-day Saint parents invest in their daughters' college education since, they assume, those girls won't have paid jobs as adults. This makes you mad. At church, you hear equally absolute and assumptive language that suggests Latter-day Saint girls won't ever want to or have to work outside the home. This makes you madder.

As your mom, I see my job in three parts: help you understand why these messages surround you, give you the confidence and tools to consider a different way, and ensure that you can hold both—the messages and your unique path—in a healthy tension while never letting anger be your calling card. As luck would have it, this may be the area of motherhood I am most qualified for.

You know I was raised in New York City as the only child of an internationally acclaimed opera singer. She had a big life. I went to school with all girls, at a place that educated us as if we were going to run a corporation or a state or even a nation someday. But your Nonna and I were also devoutly faithful, our big New York City life gathered in and made precious by our ward family. At church, like you, I received messages about the importance of my becoming a mother, but they weren't just gratuitous platitudes out of the manual. They were checked and made real by the struggles of the real-life families around me, many of which were nontraditional, as we would say today. We were all—including me and my single mother—just doing our best, and the ideal provided a guiding star that I sincerely needed as my parents fought and divorced. I didn't feel like the motherhood rhetoric I heard at church was a boundary; I felt like it was an emancipation.

That doesn't mean I stopped dreaming of my own big life. My aspirations and my tenderness for future motherhood didn't feel in conflict to me. This was partly because I had examples all around me of women who were holding both. My mother, of course. But other women too from our ward family: businesswomen, artists, educators, lawyers. Women who were also mothers and who took care of the logistical needs of family life with a wide array of tools from nannies to flexible schedules to stay-at-home fathers to live-in family members to late-stage schooling.

And so my faith and prioritization of my future family weren't pitted against my own personal development. One of the greatest gifts my mother gave me was her lack of fear that experience and adventure would dull my testimony or warp my priorities. I hope I tell you again and again: The world is a big and beautiful place. Go seize it.

Despite the vast diversity of membership and geographies and cultures that now define the Church in the twenty-first century, there is still a pervasive expectation that prioritizing motherhood has to look a particular way: specifically, good motherhood looks like mother devoting almost all her personal time and emotional resources to the nurturing of her children. I've had unique insight into this expectation: For the past ten years, I've interviewed hundreds of women around the world for the Mormon Women Project, a continuously expanding library of interviews I founded to explore the many ways Latter-day Saint women can "choose the right." I've been privy to their wrestle with this pervasive perception of motherhood. Additionally, I've worked in paying jobs almost the whole time you and your sisters have been alive, most of that time as one of the few career-building mothers I know in Utah. I myself have wrestled with how expectations match my personal choices. I've experienced and borne witness to the complicated feelings and even shame that some Latter-day Saint women experience when they work outside the home.

From my perspective, there are several fallacies intertwined in the perception that successful motherhood must be a complete dedication of time and emotional resources. The first fallacy is that women will be able *to choose* to invest complete dedication of time and emotional resources into their children. While you and I might live in a particular bubble where career-building Latter-day Saint mothers are rare, the broader truth is that most Latter-day Saint mothers cannot make that choice. Here's another fallacy: current Church leaders *want* women to offer a complete dedication of their time and emotional resources to motherhood. To be clear, that used to be taught, and many of the messages you're hearing and internalizing are residue from that prior era. In 1977 President Spencer W. Kimball sent out a call for mothers to "come home," and President Ezra Taft Benson reiterated the message in 1987.

But we believe in continuing revelation, which means that you can have utmost confidence in what our leaders are saying *now*, when they communicate directly to us today. And if what they say seems to disagree or contradict what past leaders have said, you can know that the Lord is aware of our particular day. And guess what? Today, our general leaders counsel women differently from the way general leaders counseled women in the past. "There is *no* one perfect way to be a good mother," Elder M. Russell Ballard, a member of the Church's Quorum of the Twelve Apostles, said in 2008. "Each situation is unique. Each mother has different challenges, different skills and abilities, and certainly different children. The choice is different and unique for each mother and each family."[1]

The consistent principle we can learn from the prophets' words today is not that mothers shouldn't work outside the home. It's that women's top priority should be their families. What that looks like in practice is no longer prescribed.

As you weigh the choices and paths that are right for you, with the help of personal revelation from the Lord and the prioritization of eternal truths, know that you have the support of your Church leaders. In fact, all three members of the Church's current General Relief Society Presidency have worked outside the home: Jean B. Bingham as a teacher of English as a second language to elementary students, immigrants, and refugees; Sharon Eubank as the director of LDS Charities; and Reyna I. Aburto as a translator and co-owner of a translation business with her husband.

As you take comfort in this shift in our prophets' messages, make sure you also have respect for those who chose to faithfully follow Presidents Kimball and Benson in their call to mothers to "come home." I worked professionally on the massive "I'm a Mormon" media campaign that started in 2010 with short videos profiling members of the Church in a wide variety of professional pursuits. I'll never forget the letter we received from a husband who described his wife in prostrate despondency after watching one of the videos featuring a working mom. His letter revealed the complexities of a changing church: "My wife sacrificed her education and her own ambitions to raise our children in righteousness. And now her own church's fancy PR team tells her she didn't have to do that? Now they're holding up women who deliberately disobeyed the prophet by working? My wife feels utterly betrayed."

Accompanying the fallacy that good mothers must give nearly all their time and emotional resources to their children is the belief that good motherhood has always demanded that sacrifice—that it's always been that way. That is simply not true. Just as it helps to put past leaders' counsel into historical context and to understand repercussions of inter-pretations of the counsel, so it also helps to look even farther back into history to the men and women of the early Church. They too believed families were important and that raising righteous children was a prior-ity. Nonetheless, women of Utah led in the nineteenth-century women's rights movement, not in spite of their Mormonism but because of it. Look at Emmeline B. Wells, for instance.[2] She married three times and had six children. But after outliving each of her first two husbands and then enduring, before the death of her third husband, the consequences of his financial reverses, she took responsibility to provide for herself and her five surviving children. A writer, Wells spent more than three decades as editor of the *Woman's Exponent,* a premier women's rights newspaper. She wrote thousands of editorials about women needing to reach for the educational and work opportunities that lay beyond their immediate circumstances. In her work for women, Wells became friends and colleagues with leading woman suffragists in the eastern United States, met multiple U.S. presidents, and beginning when she was eighty-two, served for eleven years as the fifth General President of the Relief Society. She lived a big life.

I hope that you, like Wells, will see the beautiful *"and"* at the center of your spiritual life. That you are a daughter of God *and* an independent spirit. That you may choose to be a future mother *and* a future business owner *and* artist *and* medical professional *and* writer *and* politician *and* teacher *and* accountant. That you can choose to do one of those things or several or something else entirely.

Some of my happiest moments are when I see you and your sisters enraptured by the big things I've pursued. You feel so serious and grown-up when I take you along to work meetings, but then you're delighted that offices can have nerf guns and free soda. You are gleeful about how "famous" I am when I'm quoted in a newspaper. We make sacrifices too. Sometimes I have to be on a call when you need homework help. Sometimes I'm distracted. I've sacrificed greater ambition to be the kind of mom I want to be. You've sacrificed having a more fully dedicated mother to support my personal development. I appreciate you for it. And I think your sacrifice has made you appreciate me too.

Ambition inherently carries with it the sacrifice of something, but the gospel teaches us how to know the right things to sacrifice.

You might be afraid that being tethered to Christ keeps you too close to home. In truth, it's just the opposite. Your membership in His Church will allow you to seek deeper and go further. Your faithfulness will free you to embrace more beauty and variety in this world than you thought possible. So go make your big life. And walk hand in hand with Christ as you do it.

NOTES

1. M. Russell Ballard, "Daughters of God," *Ensign*, May 2008.

2. See Carol Cornwall Madsen, "Emmeline B. Wells: A Fine Soul Who Served," *Ensign*, July 2003.

# I Thought I Would Take the Path More Traveled By

## JEANETTE W. BENNETT

Kenneth Linge

Jeanette Bennett's first job was at a TV station in her hometown of Idaho Falls, Idaho, where she operated a camera and made phone calls to gather weather data. She earned a bachelor's and master's degree in journalism from Brigham Young University, Provo, Utah. She founded Bennett Communications and focuses her pen on *Utah Valley Magazine*, *Utah Valley Bride Magazine*, *BusinessQ*, and *Prosper Magazine*. She and her husband, Matt, have five children.

A graduate school professor leaned across the desk and told me it would be a shame if I didn't get a PhD after finishing the master's degree I was about to complete. With a trembling heart, I told him I was four months into my first pregnancy and I didn't think additional schooling was in the cards. His disappointment was clear by his words and facial expression. He stopped his motivational speech, showed me to the door, and retrieved the brochure he had handed me for Columbia University.

I walked back to my basement apartment justifying why I had to put my dreams aside to stay home with my soon-to-be-newborn son. All the women in my sphere had stayed home, baked bread, volunteered at the PTA, scraped to put food on the table until payday, and talked very little about dreams outside the walls of their pre-Pinterest homes. I would be a stay-at-home mom like the moms, aunts, Young Women leaders, and classmates before me and beside me.

I spent the last five months of my pregnancy finishing my thesis and working as a copy editor at the *Deseret News* until twelve hours before giving birth to my 7-pound-12-ounce bundle of possibilities. I told my supervisors I might return after maternity leave but knew I didn't mean it. I accepted the path laid out by my pedigree and—I believed—by my church culture.

Labor and delivery were easier than I had been told by the women a generation ahead, and I wondered if more of my experiences would likewise differ from theirs. I rode home from our 24-hour hospital stay in the backseat so I could watch my purring newborn sleep.

With that drive home, two paths diverged in the Mormon woods, and I took the one most traveled by. After all, "The Family: A Proclamation to the World" had been revealed just four months after I exited the Idaho Falls Temple as a new bride. I envisioned one role: nurture. My less-educated but hard-working husband had three roles: provide, preside, and protect.

The only problem with my new daily life was that there was a problem: I didn't know who I was. My husband took our only car all day and into the evening so he could work two jobs. I was alone. I was lonely. I was lost. And none of this had anything to do with my feelings for my perfect baby, who sometimes required me to hold his car seat on the dryer or crinkle Walmart bags to stop his tears. I loved him. But I also wanted to love me.

I got down on my knees and asked for direction. At first, the only thing that came was peace and promise. Nothing tangible. I tried to find the answer myself. I took an evening job working at the *Idaho Falls Post Register* as a copy editor, making half my former *Deseret News* salary. I high-fived my husband when he came home for the day and I headed for my shift. I lasted only two nights. The work wasn't fulfilling, and the schedule was disruptive to our family and our marriage. What did God intend? Did he have a path for me to fulfill my divine mission as a mother with the professional life mentioned in my patriarchal blessing?

Within three months, a door to my future cracked open. My former professor at Ricks College reached out about an adjunct faculty position. With my master's degree in my back skirt pocket, I headed to Rexburg with a newly polished résumé ready for interviews. Both the English and Communications Department hired me for fall semester 1998. While I was qualified to teach freshman English, I felt unprepared for my other assignment, Communications 101: Public Speaking. As a quiet, small-town girl, I didn't consider myself a speaker.

But that teaching assignment began a realization that God was guiding my career. Two years after writing my first syllabus, I found myself speaking in front of the Utah Valley Chamber of Commerce about a new magazine publishing company I was starting. It was the first of many times I would be at a podium talking about media, women in business, following dreams, and balancing life as a Latter-day Saint woman with career ambitions.

I felt more connected to my professional colleagues and less camaraderie with women in my ward. As a young mom, I signed up to take bread to a Relief Society activity. When my bread failed to rise, I bought a loaf at the store and put it in my bread pan to carry to the stake center. I looked the other way when I heard women wonder out loud how I got the top to "curve like that." I wasn't being honest about who I was and which divine traits were truly mine.

As a thirty-one-year-old mother of four, I was called to be Young Women president in my large ward. After the sacrament meeting in which I was sustained, a woman behind me leaned up and said, "I can't believe they called a working woman." Another sister stopped me in the parking lot to say she thought the new Young Women president would be someone else, one who fit the traditional stereotype of a Latter-day Saint wife and mother.

Before the calling came, I had felt an overwhelming sense of an opportunity looming. At one point while alone in my bathroom, I said aloud, "I'll do it! Whatever it is, I'll do it!" I knew He had a spiritual task for me to complete, alongside the career for which He was guiding me. Although initially I didn't feel support from of all ward members, this calling—which I know came from God—was the start of a solid connection between my career and my faith. My executive ability came in handy as I created agendas, worked through personnel issues, resolved drama without creating more, and served alongside men. In fact, I noticed right away that some women felt uncomfortable working closely with priesthood holders in ward council. But God had prepared me through my nonspiritual experiences to sit through business board meetings and executive retreats. I knew how to voice my opinion, even if outnumbered. I knew how to lead a meeting, even if the suits outnumbered the dresses.

At times, I felt my voice was heard in the business community more than in Church settings. Sometimes men in ward leadership positions made decisions regarding the Young Women I served without consulting me. At the same time, many of my journalist colleagues from school expressed increased frustration with the Church, and some left the fold altogether.

That put me on a quest to truly articulate my testimony and my conversion to the Church, especially in regard to women's issues. I read books such as *Women at Church* by Neylan McBaine and *Women and the Priesthood* by Sheri Dew. I nodded my head in agreement through both of them and tilted my head sideways in consideration of angles I hadn't before perceived.

When I got to page 9 in Sheri's book, I got my pen out and circled and recircled a statement: "Although I can see ways in which the participation of LDS women in the Church could be further enhanced, if nothing changes in my lifetime in this regard, it won't affect my testimony one whit."

Her statement led me to stop focusing solely on ways to expand opportunities for women in the Latter-day Saint world and acknowledge truth I firmly believed in and stand steadfast. If my budget for Young Women, for example, was smaller than that given to the Young Men, I could speak up and ask for equity—but this imbalance didn't change the fact that the Book of Mormon was true. I had gained a witness that the book was from God when I finished reading it atop Hill Cumorah as a nineteen-year-old costumed pageant participant. God had also taken me by the hand and led me to teach public speaking so I could learn skills to construct and deliver a powerful talk as a business owner. I had a testimony of God and His plan for me individually and for our Church collectively. I knew what I believed and was determined to keep this as a high priority and not be distracted by cultural aspects of my faith that I thought needed enhancement.

As a thirty-six-year-old newly pregnant woman, I was again asked to lead the Young Women organization, this time as the stake Young Women president in a smoothly functioning, densely populated Utah congregation. The baby had been God's idea. And I knew the calling was too. I spent two days in tears, not because I was unhappy about the simultaneous life changes but because I wasn't sure how God could ask me to do both at once. Why did he ask the impossible?

Fortunately, I had developed a habit of going to the temple when I needed inspiration. I had fostered a love for the temple because of the clarity and power I felt from participating, especially in the women-led initiatory ordinances. When the temple opened forty-eight hours after my meeting with the stake president, I was first in line to participate in an endowment session and see if the Lord would tell me more about this dual duty. Was there a Liahona that would explain how I could add a baby and three hundred young women to my life? How could I be an effective leader in a faith where I felt, at times, less powerful than I did in the business world?

In the celestial room, I had one of those rare experiences in which I opened the Book of Mormon and found the message He needed me to hear. In Mormon 9:15 I read, "God has not ceased to be a God of miracles." That was my answer. God would perform miracles in my life so I could serve Him and His young women AND I could incorporate a fifth child into an already busy family that habitually lost book orders and ballet shoes. Through it all, I also knew He wasn't asking me to set aside my career. That was part of his continued plan for me, too.

With His promises of miracles, I marched forward and started my six-year stint as stake Young Women president, in which I felt both appreciated and, at times, muted in my calling. I was disappointed I couldn't be there when returning sister missionaries reported to the high council. These were my young women, whose testimonies I had watched grow from Beehive days into an adult ability to make eye contact and testify. I also desired autonomy to determine not only where to hold our stake girls camp but also the accompanying budget. Simply put, at times I wanted more say over the who, what, where, when, why, and how (journalistic basics) of loving my young women.

As I stewed about how I could lead out and at the same time work as an appendage to the priesthood, a quotation came to my philosophic rescue. Eliza R. Snow reportedly said of women, "Let them seek for wisdom instead of power and they will have all the power they have wisdom to exercise."[1]

My quest for me and for my young women became a search for wisdom. With my stake camp committee, I planned a stake girls camp around the theme "University of You," focused on how our Heavenly Father "who loves us and we love him" wants us to be wise, to be learned, to be prepared for whatever He calls us to do, be it public-speaking classes, budgets, and moderating debates, all the while fulfilling our other missions as women, sisters, wives, daughters, mothers. He wants us to figure out how we can love ourselves as well as those under our rooftops.

Two decades after that heart-pumping conversation during graduate school, I want to track down my graduate professor and tell him I did make something of myself. But more than that, I want to talk to that twenty-three-year-old new mom and tell her that her faith did not—and should not—hold her back from becoming all she was meant to be.

As it turns out, nurture encompasses more than motherhood. It also includes nurturing our dreams.

## NOTE

1. Eliza R. Snow, as quoted in *Daughters in My Kingdom: The History and Work of Relief Society* (Salt Lake City: The Church of Jesus Christ of Latter-day Saints, 2017), 45.

# TRIUMPH OVER TRIALS

What sound theology *can* do is to help those who
believe it to make some sense of the suffering . . . [and]
proceed with a measure of hope, courage, compassion,
and understanding of themselves even in anguish.

—*Francine R. Bennion*

# Let It Be

## PETRA CHARDON

Petra Chardon is an active member of the Utrecht Ward in the Netherlands and pianist for the ward and the Primary. She served a full-time mission and enjoys a career teaching seven- and eight-year-old children in elementary school.

Marijke Mill

As a four-year-old sitting beside my mom in a church we had never visited before, I said, "Mom, I feel at home here." It was The Church of Jesus Christ of Latter-day Saints. In the process of time my parents, siblings, and I were baptized. I felt at home there for a long time.

When I was thirteen, I discovered to my utter surprise that I had a crush on a girl I met at a Church activity. I had no idea where these feelings came from. I mentioned these feelings to no one at the time. I tried to find answers in Church literature.

Some of what I learned led me to believe that these feelings made me almost as sinful as a murderer. Because I had done nothing to invite such feelings, I was shocked and confused. I wanted to rid myself of them. The counsel in Church pamphlets was to suppress homosexual feelings and replace them with service, good thoughts, and hymns. Additionally, I was supposed to fast and pray such that my knuckles should be bloody, my head bruised, and my muscles sore or I wasn't trying hard enough for a cure.

Consequently, I dedicated my life to serving in the Church. Starting at age thirteen, I read my scriptures daily, prayed fervently, and fasted twice a month. I even transferred from a school I loved to distance myself from a girl I had a crush on. The cure didn't come. I felt like I must be failing, and my confidence faded.

At age fourteen, I visited with my bishop to discuss my frustrations. He asked if we could include my mom in our conversation. Following that discussion, my mother and I somehow decided, without exchanging a word, never to discuss the feelings again—hoping denial and suppression might heal me. By the time I was twenty, I was serving in four callings at church in an effort to enable healing.

After graduating from college, I desired to serve a mission. I hoped that the mission itself might cure me. After all, that is one of the greatest ways to serve and love God's children, according to *The Miracle of Forgiveness*. I imagined that one day while serving with my companion, the healing would miraculously take place.

I was called to the Canada Calgary Mission in 1989. I knew every word of the white handbook and was determined to be strictly obedient in hopes of being healed. Despite all my efforts, I still experienced same-sex attraction. Confused and disappointed, I thought I must be a bad person if I could not earn the right to be healed. I lived with a perpetual knot in my stomach. The doctor prescribed antidepressants, but they left me feeling disconnected from the Spirit, so I stopped taking them.

In a visit with the stake patriarch I felt loved. He mentioned me by name in the opening prayer and took time to listen to my story of struggle and confusion. He advised me to learn by heart Alma 37:37, Psalm 23, and Psalm 91. He said it was important to develop self-trust, something different from trust in the Lord. He put his hands on my head and added something to my patriarchal blessing. He never mentioned anything about my homosexual feelings changing.

Soon afterward, I met an attractive man at church. I was impressed by his scriptural knowledge and asked him to lunch. That very afternoon he asked me to marry him. I told him of my homosexual feelings. He said that with faith, God could heal me. I admired his faith and truly thought we could make it together. We were married within three months.

To my dismay I found that even in marriage, the feelings remained and even increased the harder I tried to get rid of them. In my despair I found a therapist outside the Church who taught me to acknowledge my homosexual feelings—that they didn't make me bad. The result was dramatic. The freedom to let myself feel—a freedom that I had suppressed since I was thirteen—finally returned.

My husband and I had a son, but our marriage was not a happy one. I suffered both mentally and physically. After much prayer, the answer came that it was better for us to divorce. I was deeply disappointed for failing to overcome these feelings and for giving up my dreams. If not for our two-year-old son, I never would have gotten out of bed.

Throughout this difficult process, my study gave me new insights and my perspective of Heavenly Father started to change. Before, I assumed that Heavenly Father rejected me for having homosexual feelings. But as I read the words of prophets, I started to pray in a different way. Maybe, somehow, came the thought, God understood my homosexual feelings. I received different answers—a confirmation that I was born this way and that He would lead me to find a way to deal with my homosexuality, the way I was created to find.

Even with a new relationship with God, I still had a tendency to reject myself. It had become a habit. Nevertheless, I no longer felt that my homosexual feelings needed healing. And after having fought so hard and given so much to be healed, I was so tired deep inside.

I spiraled into a period of internal chaos. I doubted everything the Church had taught, stopped studying the scriptures, and lost the sense of right and wrong. I wanted life experiences to teach me the truth. Though I questioned the very existence of God, it didn't take long before a knowledge of Him was restored. Doubting Him caused so much darkness and loneliness that it was better to believe.

I no longer felt the need to suppress my homosexual feelings. I started looking for a woman to share my life with. I wanted to express my feelings and judge them for myself. I asked to have my name removed from the records of the Church. But being excommunicated felt like I was amputated from the Church. It was painful and left me with feelings of confusion and betrayal.

But I also felt relieved not to be a member anymore. I had my own compass and didn't have to explain things. I also feared my son could be taught things in Primary that would lead him to disrespect people who are homosexual. I stayed away and hoped the Church would change.

It was difficult to find the courage to tell my parents that I was finished fighting my homosexual feelings. I feared their rejection. But they did not let me down. My father said, "Oh, you love women? So do I!" My mom and I cried together as we talked and read stories of Church members struggling through their own experiences with homosexuality. My parents' love was healing.

Soon I met a woman who was pregnant from a previous relationship. We fell in love and entered a legal partnership. While we were together, she gave birth to a daughter. It was a great joy for me to be a parent to another child, and I loved seeing my son with a little sister. Though I was anxious to accept love when I found it, I was not free from pain—especially being cut off from the Church. So I ran away.

My son and I moved back to the area where I was raised. I learned that the Church no longer took a position on the cause of same-sex attraction. I discovered that the Church no longer considers it a sin to experience homosexual feelings. These positive changes gave me hope. With this new landscape at church, I felt that I could come back.

I had missed my brothers and sisters at church. I knew I wanted to find healing and that I needed a structure to belong to, a set of rules to live by, and a group of people I could be a part of. Interestingly, it was my discovery of Buddhism before my return that put me on the path back to the Church and helped me to recognize that God wanted me there.

The bishopric, three men I knew from before my mission, lovingly assured me that there was a safe place for me and my son. We started going to church while meeting with Buddhists on alternating Sundays. The bishop extended an invitation for me to teach a Sunday School lesson on homosexuality. I thought it was so loving but didn't feel I could accept if I wasn't a member. The next morning I attended a program with my Buddhist friends and chanted with them for an hour. All the while I couldn't stop crying. I felt it was time to be baptized again. So I asked the bishop if the time was right. He was open and loving as I talked through my past with him. The bishop gave permission for the ward pianist to play "Let It Be" during the baptismal service. It felt like a warm welcome home.

Becoming a member again was difficult at first. It was painful to acknowledge that I would not be able to live in a relationship with a woman I loved. I had no idea what members might think of me and homosexuality after all those years. I hoped people would want to hear my story. However, it seemed they were frightened, and I felt doors close all around me. I stayed away some Sundays and went to the Buddhists for healing. I was so sad. I regrouped and decided to seek out the members who were accepting. I worked on forgiving the ones who had hurt me. I learned to admit to myself the pain, the anger, the disappointment, and sadness. Then I would take those feelings to God in prayer. I would let Him take care of it. I could let it go.

I feel blessed that my bishop did not wait until I was perfect to be baptized again. He accepted my willingness. My confidence has grown gradually. I still have a tendency to fall back into the old habit of thinking that I am bad. Additionally, even as I try, I am not always able to understand others. At times I cry, feeling misunderstood and censored. There are some moments at church when I can barely breathe. Even so, I feel the Spirit during Church meetings and have felt a heartwarming welcome by some members who love me for who I am. These people provide loving arms when I am sad and hurt. They speak the words that need to be said when my mouth cannot utter them. They are strong when I am weak.

Looking back I wonder if much of the therapy I've undergone would have been unnecessary if I had heard when I was young the teachings of the Church today. The impact on my emotional and physical health of those previous teachings was tremendous. However, the Lord has compensated. My son has developed into a great young man with respect for me. He served a mission and continues to thrive. My loving parents, who live such Christ-centered lives, gave me a good example and a strong base of love. Through their acceptance and example I knew deep inside that love would always win.

I love serving for its own sake and not as a tool for healing. I no longer focus on healing from homosexual feelings, which is a more joyful way of living. I know I will most likely experience homosexual feelings for the rest of my life. I accept them. It took some years of learning, healing, growing, and forgiving, but my former partner and I are now friends. That feels right. I enjoy the benefits of frequent scripture study, always reading Psalm 91 at the beginning. I recite Alma 37:37 often and recite or sing Psalm 23. I find answers through prayer and feel guided by Heavenly Father. I feel amazing healing power from members who show me the true love of Christ.

It has been extremely healing for me to write this story. In my view, there is no clear answer for the way a person who experiences same-sex attraction should live. My story is not intended to show that my way is the only way. I have seen people make decisions that were completely different from mine. Some are not happy, and others are! Some are still seeking more answers. I have come to realize that it is important for people to find out for themselves what their mission is and what works for them.

We are put here on this earth for a reason. Some parts of the journey must be done alone, without the help of other human beings. But God is always with us, whether we feel Him or not. Many parts of our journey, however, can be done beside someone else. We can share and learn and uplift and be uplifted. That is all part of the gospel. The Saviour loves us all. He understands our personal needs and knows our hearts and minds. We are safe with Him.

# Healed by Love

## DEANNA GOURLEY

Nicole Stoker

Deanna Gourley was born in Buffalo, New York, and was baptized into The Church of Jesus Christ of Latter-day Saints when she was sixteen years old. She graduated from Brigham Young University, Provo, Utah, with a degree in marriage and family development and served as a Spanish-speaking missionary in Houston, Texas. She is married to Jason Gourley and has five beautiful children, including one with severe disabilities. She lives in Lehi, Utah, and is a stay-at-home mom.

Since finding and joining the Church, I have come to know what family and the Savior's perfect love really mean. My earliest memories are of abuse toward me and my siblings. For example, sometime when I was a toddler, I remember my father and mother yelling and fighting. In a fit of rage, my father threw my infant brother across the room. When I was five years old, I got off the school bus excited to see my mother waiting for me on the porch. She grabbed me by my hair, dragged me into the house, and threw me into my room. I had left my room messy, and because she did not let go of my hair when she threw me, I paid for my mistake with the globs of hair left behind in her hands. Finally, as an eight year old, after having a weekend visit with my father, I was told he wanted nothing more to do with me because I was overweight.

Needless to say, I didn't feel loved or accepted by my mother or my father. As I grew older, my friends invited me to attend church with them; however, I came away feeling even more scared and alone. These churches were mostly Protestant or Catholic and seemed to teach of a God who punished us and made us spend an eternity in hell.

By the time I was sixteen years old, I felt alone, unwanted, and useless. I thought about dying and wondered if anyone would even notice I was gone. Eventually, I spoke with friends about killing myself, and they notified the school's guidance counselor. Instead of giving me help, he told me to stop seeking attention and called my mother, who consequently beat me in response to her having been disturbed by the school. Several weeks passed. The tension, emptiness, and helplessness increased. I tried turning to alcohol and boys for acceptance and love, but that only made me feel worse.

My life changed one Saturday evening in May 1996. My mother was getting ready to go out drinking, a common activity for her. I was downstairs, cleaning a room and taking care of my five-year-old sister. My mother called me to come help her find her shoe. As I walked up the stairs, I let out a typical teenager sigh. Upon hearing that, my mother came unglued. She chased me down the stairs, yelling at me and telling me, "You are an ungrateful, selfish child. I never, ever wanted you." She continued, "You are dead to me, and I never want anything to do with you again." These words to an already broken child were an invitation to end my life. That's exactly what I planned to do.

After my mother left for the night, I finished my cleaning and put my little sister to bed. I went downstairs to the kitchen to end my misery. At this point, the fear of God's wrath and punishment was less painful than continuing to live with a woman who should have loved me but seemed to hate me.

The kitchen was dark, with only a little light coming from a nearby night-light. I grabbed the sharpest knife I could find and held it to my wrist. While I was trying to cut myself, the knife fell from my hands. I picked it up even more determined. Again the knife fell. I tried a third time, this time gripping harder. The knife should have cut my vein, but once more, it fell to the ground. At this point, I dropped to the floor, too, and cried. I did not understand what was happening but realized that suicide was not the answer. Looking back on it after all these years, I don't know why I was stopped in my attempts when so many others aren't, but I do *know* that it was Heavenly Father stopping me. It was as if He were saying, "No! Don't give up! There is another way."

Eventually, I picked myself up off the floor and called a friend who allowed me to stay with her and her family for a couple of days. That night I started a journey toward what would eventually lead me to the most rewarding gift: divine love and acceptance from a Heavenly Father and Heavenly Mother who want nothing less than for me to feel Their love and return to live with Them again!

After a couple of days of staying with my friend, I called a social worker who had been working with my family. I explained to her what had happened and, although it is not typical, she allowed me to live with her and her two sons as a foster daughter. It was in her home that I learned about The Church of Jesus Christ of Latter-day Saints. I attended church with her and her family. I was surprised that they didn't teach of a mean God but of a loving God. For several months, I continued to learn about the Church and its teachings and decided to be baptized in October. I can't say I had a real testimony of anything, but I knew there was something different being taught. I felt safer within this church than I had anywhere else. By March, my foster mother had her own issues and decided she couldn't handle a broken teenager as well. To my surprise, she dropped me off at a homeless shelter for youth. Even though I felt betrayed by her then, I have come to realize that her gift to me was introducing me to the gospel of Jesus Christ.

Nevertheless, this fresh abandonment came as a blow to me. Why was I so unlovable? How could so many people just throw me away? All I ever wanted was to be loved and to be part of a family. I didn't understand all of the whys and wondered if I would ever feel loved or even worthy of having such a privilege.

After four months at the shelter, I rented a room from a family in my branch during my senior year of high school. I still felt alone and unwanted, but deep down something kept pushing me forward. I was not yet able to understand what the pushing was, but I continued surviving. I graduated from high school and was accepted into Brigham Young University. It was there, during my freshman year, that I began to see and feel that I was both loved and wanted and that I did have a family: a Heavenly Family.

My friend and Relief Society president at BYU, challenged me to get up and share my testimony in church. We frequently discussed my fear that Heavenly Father didn't love me and that He would eventually let me down just as everyone else had. She promised me that if I bore my testimony, I would feel His love. Reluctantly, I decided to take the challenge. I don't remember what I said, but immediately upon finishing, I felt overwhelmed. I felt I had shared too much and made myself too vulnerable. I walked to the restroom to escape and experienced something I had never felt before. I felt love. It scared me! I tried to run! I locked myself in a stall and fell to the floor in the fetal position. But the feeling didn't go away. It's hard to explain what happened next. Though I was alone, I felt Heavenly Father's arms around me. Holding me. Loving me. I heard Him whisper into my heart, "I love you! I always have, and I always will! Let Me in, let My Son into your heart, and you will find what you have been looking for. But I know you need time, so I will be here waiting for you with my arms ready to wrap you in my protection."

I knew it would take time. I needed to do the work necessary to reverse the negative consequences of a lifetime of emotional, physical, and spiritual abuse. I started going to therapy. I began to really study my scriptures and build a relationship with my Heavenly Parents and Their Son, Jesus Christ. As I learned of the Atonement, I realized that Jesus Christ is the only One who knows what I felt and experienced growing up. He knows the anguish caused by hearing you are unlovable and unacceptable because of how you look. He knows the despair that drives someone to want to end it all because life is just too unbearable. That is pure love! How can our Heavenly Parents *not* love us? They allowed Their Son to be abused, beaten, and left for dead so that no one would ever have to fight any earthly battle alone. I learned by accepting Their love that I was part of a family—a heavenly family—who would never disown me.

There are times today, years later, when I find myself having what I refer to as a "Laman and Lemuel experience." Laman and Lemuel, the two older sons of Lehi the prophet, continued to murmur and were quick to forget all that the Lord had done for them and shown to them—even after they saw an angel of the Lord and witnessed miracles in their lives (1 Nephi 3:31). Likewise, when trials and hardships are placed on my back, sometimes I revert to my old self and pull away from God and His love. That leaves me feeling abandoned, unloved, and more likely to doubt the experiences that have taught me the truths about my Heavenly Parents and Jesus Christ. Yet, the beautiful thing is that truths never change. Heavenly Father and Heavenly Mother will always patiently wait for me. I know that They and Their Son understand when my heart needs time to catch up with my brain. Their arms are continually outstretched to me, ready to welcome me home and wrap me in Their love. That is what happens in the best families and, most assuredly, in our Heavenly Family! That is what I want to instill in my relationships with others and especially with my own children.

As I raise my children, I emphasize that we need to love one another and to show that love daily for each other. My hope is that my children, and others with whom I come in contact, will know that they are loved and wanted, regardless of what they do or how they look. Love is a basic right, not something to be earned. Genuine love is something that is freely given and can't be taken away. And it isn't something we can fake. Love is natural and pure when it comes from Christ. Our love for one another needs to mimic Jesus's love. That's when it matters most! Over time, I have learned to show love with my whole self by giving of myself completely—trying to love as Jesus did. And perhaps, when others see and feel my love, they will more easily be able to feel and accept the perfect love of Heavenly Parents and Jesus Christ.

As difficult and heart-wrenching as my childhood and adolescence were, I would not change what I experienced. The lessons I learned and the people who crossed my path molded me into the woman I am today. I choose to end the cycle of abuse and abandonment. I choose to be an example of love to all I meet. And I choose to create a family that is patient and participates in the pure love of Christ.

# Getting Better, Not Even

NAME WITHHELD

I really want to tell you my name, show you my photo, and say something about myself, but I have chosen, for now, to write as Name Withheld. I am proud of the hard work I have done as a survivor of sexual abuse, and I continue to heal every day. By not revealing my identity or the identity of the abuser, I hope to allow him space to acknowledge and properly deal with his abusive behavior and not to cause a rift within my extended family.

The first feeling was guilt. Then came shame, self-loathing, anger, worthlessness, confusion, and loneliness. Sometimes it was more than I could handle. I screamed into a towel to muffle the sound, tried to fight the memories, and prayed that the horror would disappear. As a college student, I'm still struggling to understand what happened and why it happened to me.

I had felt uncomfortable around a certain family member for years, but I couldn't seem to figure out why. Then #MeToo happened. Women across the world spoke up about their experiences with sexual harassment, sexual abuse, and sexual assault. Some of their stories seemed familiar to me, and I often connected with an experience or feeling they shared. And then I started to understand. The memories I had buried in the back of my mind started to come to the surface—memories of having been sexually abused as a child.

When children are abused, their brains sometimes lock away the memory until the child is better able to cope with the trauma. That is what happened to me. A few years after the abuse ended, memories began to surface, and flashbacks made their frequent appearance. I began reliving my childhood trauma as a teenager who now understood a little more about what was happening in my flashbacks. I realized that whenever he had made me feel special, he was just manipulating me.

Sometimes the flashbacks were so vivid I couldn't tell where I currently was or who was in the room with me. Back in my younger body, I would try to run away or call for help, but I wasn't able to make a sound in that version of reality. Other times, I was older and watching the abuse, fully aware of what was happening. I tried to take the little girl's hand and gently lead her away, telling her that she would be safe somewhere else. But I was never able to to do that.

Recalling these instances, I felt afraid and alone. The confusion and strain from trying to fill in the gaps in my memory and understand everything that had occurred made me often doubt myself. Was it possible that it was all just a bad dream? To complicate things more for my teenage brain, my abuser was and still is an active member of The Church of Jesus Christ of Latter-day Saints. He served a full-time mission, married in the temple, and has two young children. In my mind, it didn't make sense that a member of my extended family, and a member of my faith, could be responsible for such actions. I wanted to tell someone what had happened to me, but I was scared. What if no one believed me? Would I be branded as a troublemaker, a liar, or even mentally unstable?

Sundays were hard days. The topics of sexual abuse and sexual assault were rarely mentioned in my church experience. I would look at the girls sitting next to me in my Young Women class and wonder if any of them had suffered abusive experiences like mine. My friends talked about looking forward to family reunions and spending fun-filled days with their grandparents, aunts, uncles, and cousins. I felt I was the only girl who got anxious about seeing some members of my extended family and subconsciously looked over my shoulder at family gatherings, worried that the wrong person might be too close. The girls talked about the blessings they had noticed in their lives from living the law of chastity; I stayed quiet in my uncomfortable feelings of confusion and guilt. I wanted to ask questions and confirm my worthiness, but how could I? How would the girls and leaders in my ward react if they knew about my past? So I stayed silent and remained an outsider with a horrible secret.

With such an emphasis on marriage in Latter-day Saint doctrine and culture, I often wondered who would want to marry me. Did I lose my virtue as a child? I imagined someone saving money for years to buy a car. I imagined him going to a dealership, admiring all the shiny cars, and then seeing a beat-up, rusty car. Who would choose that car when when all the perfectly clean vehicles were available? Of course, I was the dirty and undesirable car. I was nothing more than a disposable object, used and then thrown away. Didn't every righteous man want to marry a pure, virtuous woman who is clean, unblemished, and innocent? Isn't that what every chastity lesson in Sunday School and Young Women classes had taught me?

I also felt I was too radical for my Young Women group. No one else seemed to care passionately about women's issues the way I did. The female battle for safety and respect had become personal, and I was determined to speak up about such taboo topics as sexual abuse. Sometimes I felt I was outspoken. But was I? Maybe everyone else was just quiet.

The #MeToo movement was what pushed me to finally open up about the abuse. I was inspired by women around the world who were speaking up. I intently followed the International Women's March and realized that there were girls and women all over the world like me! They were battling mental monsters just as I was, and they were overcoming. I realized I wanted that for myself. Still, I was terrified to tell my parents what had happened to me. Just thinking about telling them made me feel sick to my stomach. And what if I started a war within my extended family by speaking up? I was afraid that I would ruin my family. I knew that my parents loved me and wanted the best for me, but telling them about being sexually abused terrified me. I worried that my parents wouldn't believe me, or might be ashamed of me, or would even be angry with me. I now understand how irrational, but normal, all of those thoughts were. As happens with many other victims, however, fear kept me quiet for quite some time.

Finally, though, I found the courage to tell my parents about some of the childhood memories and a little about the flashbacks and nightmares I was experiencing. They were surprised and sad but responded with love, concern, and, to my relief, belief. They assured me that the abuse was not my fault and that they would do everything they could to help me heal. My parents found an excellent therapist who worked specifically with childhood trauma issues.

After several months of therapy, my therapist and I decided it would be beneficial for me to meet with my abuser and tell him that I remembered being abused as a young child. In a way, I wanted to hand the sordid past to him and, in my mind at least, continue moving on with my life without the painful attachment to him. The abuser denied any wrongdoing and spluttered out illogical and contradicting statements in an attempt to assert his innocence. My therapist had prepared me well for his response, and I felt strong as I looked him in the eye and told him in clear terms that no matter how many times he denied it, the abuse had still happened.

During my months of therapy, life for me was slowly getting better, but then, unexpectedly, waves of depression, fear, and guilt would crash over me, trying to drown me in the memories and pain from my childhood experiences. The nightmares were more vivid than ever, and the flashbacks haunted me. When my therapist asked me how I was feeling, I would reply "shattered," "destroyed," or "dead." On some days, the emotional pain was so severe that I hid in my room. Other days, numbness left me thinking that it didn't matter what happened to me because I was just a body, an object. I was angry at my abuser for a long time. He had caused me pain, he had made me feel worthless. He had used me as an object.

The hardest part of healing from the abuse was the constant feeling of unworthiness. For a long time, I was confused about the meaning of virtue. I learned through therapy, talking with my parents, and carefully studying and praying about the topic that virtue is not like a chest of rubies. Virtue cannot be stolen. Virtue is about consent—my consent. My purity and worthiness before God is strictly between Him and me. The abuse I survived as a child cannot ever decrease my worthiness. The actions of another cannot take away my virtue.

I often asked God how He could seemingly sit back and watch that happen to a child. I pleaded with Him for some sort of understanding, peace, and confirmation that the abuse was not my sin. Despite knowing better, I still often felt I was responsible in some way for what had happened. I still saw myself as unclean and unworthy. I felt there was a great distance between me and Heaven that I couldn't bridge. Why didn't He help me during those times of awful abuse? Why was I suffering so much now for something I hadn't wanted, hadn't consented to, and hadn't even understood? Was I important to God? Did He even care about me anymore?

On hard days, I received many simple gifts of help. When I felt lonely and afraid, a friend felt prompted to send a thoughtful text. When I felt depressed, I was guided to a scripture or general conference address that contained exactly what I needed. When I was confused or sad or exhausted, my mother sat with me for hours as I talked or sobbed or expressed no emotion at all. When I was terrified at night, my father lovingly gave me a priesthood blessing and stayed with me until I calmed down. All of these small tender mercies reminded me that I was loved and still had value. As I embarked on a serious study of Jesus Christ and His love for me, I realized how intimately Christ understood my six-year-old self and my current self.

This childhood trauma is now part of my life. Of course, I wish it were different, but the coping and adaptive skills I have obtained through years of therapy have strengthened me and will help me as I take on other challenges in the future. Through these trials, I have learned to rely on the love and grace of Jesus Christ. I have regained my confidence in attending my church meetings and voicing my thoughts. I have been able to connect with other survivors and have drawn strength from their courage, resilience, and faith. Certainly there are still hard days ahead, but I feel better equipped now to confidently make valuable contributions to my family, my church, and the world. I am learning that my life is about getting better, not getting even.

## A NOTE FROM MOM:

This is my daughter's story, and I love her, support her, and applaud her courage in sharing her painful experience of childhood sexual abuse. We both recognize that every situation of sexual harassment, sexual abuse, and sexual assault is different, and each survivor has the right to determine her path of healing. My daughter's healing story is hers, and your healing experience doesn't have to happen in the same way.

If you have experienced abuse of any kind, please know you are not alone, that many others are right this minute on a journey to healing, and you can begin your own healing journey at Abuse.ChurchofJesusChrist .org or by contacting your local crisis support hotline for immediate help.

# CONTINUED EDUCATION

Let us open the books of life and salvation and
study also the great authors, poets, and painters,
that our minds may be clothed with intelligence
and our hearts abound with human feeling.

—*Bathsheba W. Smith*

# Make It Your Own

## KATE HARLINE

Courtesy of the author

Kate Harline lives in Salt Lake City, Utah, with her husband, Brian Andelin, and daughter, Matilda. She earned a bachelor's degree in religious studies from Seattle Pacific University, Seattle, Washington, served a mission in southern France, and has a master's degree in social work from the University of Utah, Salt Lake City, Utah. As a licensed clinical social worker, Kate has worked in a domestic violence shelter, as a school social worker, on Utah's suicide prevention hotline, as a therapist in private practice, and as a therapist for refugees who are survivors of torture.

I remember the day I found out my life's calling was off-limits.

It was during my freshman year of college at Seattle Pacific University in a class called Career Development. In the class I took an extensive test meant to help me discover what fields of study and work would be most fulfilling for me based on my personality and strengths. I couldn't wait to get the test back to find out what my future might hold. I excitedly turned to the page that revealed my results and read the top result: *Pastor/Priest/Minister.*

Well, unless I wanted to change religions, this particular vocation was not available to me as a woman. But twelve years later, I've come to realize that the career match test hadn't been so far off and that my life calling wasn't off-limits after all—I just had to "make it my own." I went on to major in religious studies, serve a full-time mission in France, and get a master's degree in social work. All of these have felt a lot like being a pastor/priest/minister—especially my career as a clinical social worker.

Religious leaders minister to their congregants, listen to their problems, help them find solutions, advocate on their behalf, connect them to needed resources, care about them, and treat them with compassion. These are the same sorts of things I do as a social worker.

This can mean being a listening ear on the suicide prevention hotline for someone who feels hopeless, or helping a single mother from

North Korea deal with the effects of the ongoing trauma she experienced while living in that oppressive state, or trying to track down a desperate and alcoholic client who has been evicted from his apartment. This can mean listening as a client from a war-torn country in Africa describes what it was like to see her son killed, or going to visit a client who's been hospitalized because her hallucinations and delusions made her a danger to herself, or helping an Iraqi woman understand what rights a woman has in the United States against an abusive spouse. This can mean driving to a client's home to take her diapers for her baby because her husband's income is barely enough to cover the monthly rent, or helping a transgender boy find ways to cope with anxiety and depression. This can also mean providing emotional support to an eleventh-grade girl who finds herself pregnant and then providing additional emotional support when she has a miscarriage, or counseling with a young Latter-day Saint woman who is experiencing a faith crisis.

Yes, it feels an awful lot like my own version of being a pastor/priest/minister, and I really love it.

In my thirty years of life thus far, it has worked well for me to try to "make it my own" when it comes to life choices. What I think this really comes down to is trying to live consciously. To be conscious means to be awake. It means living intentionally, deliberately, knowingly, willfully, and on purpose. The more conscious I have been in choosing how to live my life, the more fulfilled I have found myself to be. I've also noticed that among my therapy clients—when they take ownership of their life and choices, they feel a much stronger sense of self-sufficiency and well-being.

I recently gave birth to my first child. Becoming a mother is a major life event that definitely requires conscious choices. Do I want to be a mother? What does it mean to be a mother? What does it look like, sound like, feel like? The truth is that every woman must answer these questions for herself—she must "make it her own." The problem comes when a woman sees the way someone else does it and assumes that she must do it the same way.

A female Latter-day Saint client told me recently, "I've decided I don't want to have children. I went to visit my friend who has three kids and she seemed miserable. Her husband is gone all day, and she's with these three young kids all by herself, and she's totally depressed." My response to her was, "That's fine if you decide you don't want kids, but my question is, Is that what having kids has to look like?"

My answer is NO! Do it how it works for you. Make it your own!

When my husband, Brian, and I decided that we wanted to have a child, we were unsure exactly how to answer such questions as, Who will take care of the baby during the day? Who will make money so we can afford to live? Who will advance their career? As it turns out, I get a lot of joy from taking care of our daughter, Matilda—and so does Brian. And Brian gets a lot of fulfillment from his career—and I get a lot of fulfillment from mine. And so we have tried to "make it our own" and consciously choose arrangements that work for both of us. For example, for the first six months of Matilda's life, we were able to have this arrangement: in the mornings, I would go to work, and Brian would care for Matilda; in the afternoons, Brian would go to work, and I would take care of her. For those months, being "equal partners," as "The Family: A Proclamation to the World" says, meant truly dividing things equally.

My father is a history professor at Brigham Young University. Especially during the years when there were few female faculty, various female students said to him, "I love history and I would love to pursue a master's degree or a PhD in history . . . but I also want to be a mom." My dad (while wishing there were more female professors to say it instead) usually said something like, "The more education you get, the more qualified you'll be for a variety of good jobs, which will mean more flexibility in your schedule and probably leave you feeling more personally fulfilled—all of which will probably help you be a happier and better parent." I've found that advice to be true for me. Following that advice has also resulted in more parity between my husband and me—because Brian and I have equal schooling and qualifications, we have the same earning power. That means that as different seasons in life arise, we can have flexibility about how to share the responsibilities of work and family. Also, to my father's students, I would add that it should go without saying that contributing to the world as a mother and contributing to the world in other ways are not mutually exclusive endeavors!

Life is full of exciting opportunities, and women and girls have more possibilities open to them now than ever before. There's no one way to live life as a woman! Our Heavenly Parents know better than any career match test how our individual gifts and talents can be used to better the world. We have the privilege to seek our own illumination about how to consciously "make it your own" when it comes to family, career, and so many other aspects of life.

# My Wild God

## MICHELLE LEE

Carrie George

Michelle Lee is a licensed therapist based in Palo Alto, California. She is the daughter, sister, and aunt to a family of amazing people. Michelle loves anything related to psychology, philosophy, reading good books, running, and photography. She is happiest when standing among the Rocky Mountains of her native Canada.

As I write this, I am just a few months shy of my fortieth birthday. Life at this stage feels like a whirlwind of kinetic energy. I feel a bit like I'm halfway through a good novel, in which the characters and setting are already fairly well established but there is still plenty of time for a few more plot twists. I still feel the energy of youth, and yet I am also starting to see doors that were previously open to me begin to close. I'm beginning to notice the grief of missed opportunities and feel more keenly the knowledge that I cannot have everything that I might have loved. Every season of life has its wisdom, I think, and part of the wisdom of this particular season comes from being placed squarely in the middle of different tensions—life and death, love and loss, safety and risk, belonging and loneliness.

I think about these tensions a lot, although, truth be told, this is not a new thing for me. My Latter-day Saint upbringing was thoroughly conventional, or at least it seemed so at the time (though I now know that nobody's story is ever simple), and as a youth I fully expected to follow the path laid out for me, which was heavily focused on marriage and motherhood. Life brought me neither of those things, as it turns out. I have felt all kinds of different emotions about that (sadness, grief, shame, joy, excitement, gratitude, to name a few), but the story I want to tell here is less about how to grapple with being single and childless as a Latter-day Saint woman and more about how having your expectations shattered can open your eyes to possibilities and joys that you otherwise would never have considered.

I think humans are wired to seek certainty, and we do this whenever we set expectations for how our lives are "supposed to" unfold. I see this all the time as a therapist who works with anxiety disorders. After all, anxiety is, in essence, an unhealthy obsession with safety and certainty, and effectively managing it is not about learning to be *more certain* so much as it is about learning to be *brave,* even in the face of risk. It is true that if you live too much within a state of groundless uncertainty, you are likely to feel lost and without direction or purpose. As I was growing up, most of my Church lessons were geared toward helping me avoid those pitfalls—and honestly, that was probably helpful for me as a child. But when the expectations for my own life did not materialize in the way I was promised, it forced me to reconsider the belief that living a certain way ("righteously," I would have said) meant that I could expect certain specific results. No matter how I live, though, there is always risk.

That was a really uncomfortable realization, and for a time I didn't know what to do with it. One experience has continually been a source of strength on my own faith journey, and I've gone back to it again and again over the intervening years. One night when I was twenty-three years old and in my first semester of graduate school, I knelt beside my bed and began pouring out my heart to God. At the time, I was just starting to have an inkling that my life might not follow the path I had expected, and I was both terrified and excited (although I would not really admit the excitement to myself until years later). So I prayed, and I told God my deepest and barely acknowledged hopes and fears and asked—desperately—for godly acceptance and understanding. I have not received many answers from God before or since, but that night I did, and I think my impressions of that response have continued to evolve as I have. What I felt from God was a sense of acceptance, but more than that, I felt delight, and wildness, and a deep respect for my agency as an individual. It was as though God were saying to me, "These are good desires. Your life is yours, and I will walk with you and help you create, as I do." I felt it was a covenant between us, and it has been the most binding covenant of my life.

Years later, I came across a quote from the great poet Rainer Maria Rilke, taken from a letter written to a young student. In the letter, Rilke implores his protégé to "have patience with everything unresolved in your heart. Try to love the *questions themselves*, like locked rooms and like books written in a foreign language. . . . It is a question of experiencing everything. At present, you need to *live* the question. Perhaps you will gradually, without even noticing it, find yourself experiencing the answer, some distant day."[1] I recognize in Rilke's words something of the same God who spoke to me that night. To truly *live* the questions means not only *tolerating* the anxiety of the unknown, but actively *leaning into it* with both acceptance and hope.

Life has not always brought me what I expected. But in allowing myself to let go of the life I had planned and accept and thrive in the life that God and I have created together, I find myself continually surprised and delighted by what it has to offer. This has been true in regard to my own life plans, but it has also been true anytime I had to confront anything new and difficult and unsettling. There is sometimes pain and grief, yes, and sometimes I need to summon my own bravery to face its darkness. But I love this life.

My testimony, paradoxically, exists within all these tensions, somewhere in the space between knowing and not-knowing. I freely admit that church is often difficult for me, because so much of modern Latter-day Saint worship is about testifying to the certain truth of a particular story, and I am not, by nature or experience, inclined toward certainty. For this reason, my activity in the Church has waxed and waned at different points in my life, sometimes for years. But even so, I have found many fellow travelers along this road and know there is still space for those of us who not only explore these borderlands but relish the struggle. And I have not let myself lose the wild God that struggles with me.

I think about Eve sometimes and picture her face as she leaves the garden and fixes her gaze determinedly toward the lone and dreary world she is about to enter. I think she understands both the fear and the exhilaration that come from facing the unknown. I think she understands that while strong convictions are necessary to direct our path, uncertainty and risk and vulnerability are the engines of growth itself. I believe she is brave. I believe she is all of us.

## NOTE

1. Rainer Maria Rilke and Franz Xaver Kappus, *Letters to a Young Poet*, trans. M.D. Herter Norton (New York: W. W. Norton & Co., 1993).

# I Never Planned to Go to Divinity School

## JANIECE JOHNSON

Janiece Johnson has master's degrees in American religious history and theology from Brigham Young University, Provo, Utah, and Vanderbilt University, Nashville, Tennessee, respectively, and a doctorate from the University of Leicester, Leicester, England. She is general editor of the *Mountain Meadows Massacre: Complete Legal Papers* and coauthor of *The Witness of Women: Firsthand Experiences and Testimonies of the Restoration.* She is a research associate at the Neal A. Maxwell Institute for Religious Scholarship at BYU.

Growing up as a Latter-day Saint in California, I didn't really know what divinity school was. I wasn't going to be ordained as a minister—why would a Latter-day Saint girl do such a thing?

Yet, here I was, driving to Nashville, Tennessee, ready to begin divinity school at Vanderbilt University.

This was one of many critical times in my life that I've had to rely on the Spirit and step (sometimes leap) into the darkness. I didn't know anyone who had gone to divinity school; no one had said, "This is what you should do." I needed the Spirit to show me that this was my path. I remembered Elder Neal A. Maxwell saying, "The Holy Ghost will preach to you from the pulpit of memory" in a regional conference at Brigham Young University.[1] Sometime later, a professor suggested that Vanderbilt might be a good place for me. That thought kept coming back to me. I followed the glimmer of inspiration, and it led me to Nashville.

I had a vague worry that academic notions of religion might be harmful to my testimony. Ever the planner, I strategized that I would listen to conference talks on my way to and from school each day as an antidote to whatever spirit-crushing things I had learned that day. I also worried that all my Latter-day Saint marriage possibilities were being left behind in Utah. Despite my concerns, I very clearly felt that I was supposed to go to Vanderbilt.

My initial worries weren't unfounded—religion and the academy can maintain an uncomfortable coexistence, but the tension can also be productive. I had been well prepared by academically centered religion classes at BYU and had already begun to consider difficult questions of the gospel and scriptural text. Some things came easier than others. My first semester I took classes in early Christianity, Hebrew Bible, and American religious history. When my early Christianity professor showed us archeological photographs of ancient baptismal fonts not used for the living, I joked that the Latter-day Saints knew just what to do with those. I marveled at differences amongst Christians, how we define authority and interpret scripture. I also recognized that all religious people are not on the same side of the political aisle. When some of my evangelical friends struggled to face the historical reality of man-made scripture that took hundreds of years to come together as a biblical canon, the Book of Mormon had already taught me that any text will be limited by the "mistakes of men."[2] I came to believe that the limitations of the scriptural text do not negate their spiritual value; they just complicate it. Joseph Smith taught that mortal language is always limited—"crooked, broken, scattered, and imperfect."[3] Despite that, the imperfect medium of language can be a conduit to revelatory transcendence if combined with the Spirit. I began to love the beauty of the Bible, sometimes even because of its human limitations.

During my second semester at Vanderbilt, I took a feminist theology class. As a student at BYU, I had read a *BYU Studies* article, "Feminism in Light of the Gospel of Jesus Christ," and my response was pretty basic: Jesus was a feminist, and so am I. As Mary Stovall Richards and B. Kent Harrison wrote, "In its most basic form, feminism echoes eternal truths of the gospel, which affirms the equal worth of all people, the equal right to and capacity for spirituality, and the evils of abuse."[4] I never understood those who saw *feminism* as a bad word; however, in my feminist theology class, I learned that patriarchy was *the* great evil in the world. And there came the tension. I grew up in an egalitarian family and ward and until that point I had really only seen the good that came from a patriarchal church structure. I had always been able to write off aberrations from the good as corrupt individuals—individuals who were "set . . . upon the things of this world, and aspire[d] to the honors of men" who could no longer lay claim on priesthood authority no matter their position (Doctrine and Covenants 121:35–37). Within that structure I had been loved, taken care of, and given opportunities to thrive.

I read from cutting-edge feminist theologians and saw many parallels to Latter-day Saint theology. Focusing on the feminine Divine might have been radical for those Protestant and Catholic theologians, but Joseph Smith was radical. Elements of Latter-day Saint theology have always been radical. I entered the class believing I had both a Heavenly Mother and a Heavenly Father. I could see the expansive potential of our doctrine and the importance of women in fulfilling that vision. Equality was not something to dismiss because of contemporary political baggage. Equality was central to the law of consecration and central to the restored gospel. For the first time, I really began to contemplate why the Lord said, "If ye are not equal in earthly things ye cannot be equal in obtaining heavenly things" (Doctrine and Covenants 78:6). If we were to become "equal in power, and in might, and in dominion" in the celestial kingdom, then "equality among all" had to become our goal here (Doctrine and Covenants 76:95; Mosiah 27:3).

I could not dismiss the good that I had seen in the Church, nor could I dismiss the difficulties that were opening up before my eyes as I began to more deeply consider the experiences of others. Reading womanist and liberation theologies helped me to consider the effect of racial and economic differences. I recognized that not everyone has the privilege to brush off what I saw as aberrations; for some, that is all they experience. Latter-day Saint theology taught me that every soul was of infinite worth in the sight of God, and feminist theology reminded me that I needed to work so that all souls were valued and could thrive. If we value the souls of others as does God, then we must take that important first step to listen to their voices.

My time at Vanderbilt pushed me and stretched me in ways that were not always comfortable. Yet, I consistently gained more confidence in the beautiful and radical nature of our religion as I grew increasingly grateful for the Book of Mormon, the Bible, and perhaps most significantly, revelation.

Negotiating a space between academic arguments and gospel truths requires the guidance of the Spirit. Finding a place as an academic, single woman in a married church requires the guidance of the Spirit. Knowing when to speak up and when to shut my mouth requires the guidance of the Spirit. Relief Society General President Julie Beck said, "The ability to qualify for, receive, and act on personal revelation is the single most important skill that can be acquired in this life."[5] I believe she spoke an essential truth. Again and again, my own experience has underscored this truth: If I can confidently stand before God, I will be okay. But I must learn to hear God's voice. The Lord speaks to me after my "manner of . . . language" so that I "might come to understanding" (Doctrine and Covenants 1:24). As I continue to gain this skill, I learn the pattern that the Lord uses to communicate with me. No one else could perfectly tell me how to learn that; I have to learn through my own experience.

When I first arrived in my apartment in Nashville, I remember thinking, "I'm not moving until I have a PhD in hand." I knew I needed a PhD, and here I was—ready. So, A plus B must equal C, right? Yet, a year later, I decided I would not stay to complete a PhD there but would leave with a master's of theology. That decision was more difficult than going in the first place, but again, I felt certain of my course. It was not the final step in my schooling, as I had anticipated. Rather, it was an essential step along the way. At that point, I could not imagine that it would take another decade until I would complete my PhD. I had a glimpse of where I was headed; I just didn't expect the path it would require.

My time at Vanderbilt is representative of a consistent theme in my life: My life follows a circuitous path. I mostly believe that circles are way more interesting than straight lines, but I still sometimes wish my life proceeded in a more straightforward way. Nevertheless, I have been guided all along the way. In the middle of one of those winding paths, Camille Fronk Olson commented to me that many faithful women she knows lead circuitous lives. Sometimes I'm able to let go of my expectations and frustrations to really see the beauty of my path. As I look back, I can see value in all the circles. And in quiet moments, I'm overwhelmed by the grace and the guidance I receive along the way.

## NOTES

1. See Neal A. Maxwell, "Willing to Submit," *Ensign*, May 1985.

2. Title Page, Book of Mormon: Another Testament of Jesus Christ (Salt Lake City: The Church of Jesus Christ of Latter-day Saints, 2013).

3. "Letter to William W. Phelps, 27 November 1832," p. 2, *The Joseph Smith Papers*, http://www .josephsmithpapers.org/paper-summary/letter-to-william-w-phelps-27-november-1832/2.

4. Mary Stovall Richards and B. Kent Harrison, "Feminism in the Light of the Gospel of Jesus Christ," *BYU Studies Quarterly* 36, no. 2 (1996):181.

5. Julie B. Beck, "And upon the Handmaids in Those Days Will I Pour Out My Spirit," *Ensign*, May 2010.

# LEARNING BY STUDY AND ALSO BY FAITH

To know the fundamental truths of the gospel is to leave one free to go far and wide, anchored by that knowledge, in search of all else that earth and sea and skies have to teach.

—*Elsie Talmage Brandley*

# "I'm the Bishop!" and Other Reflections

## DEIDRE NICOLE GREEN

Deidre Nicole Green is a postdoctoral fellow at the Neal A. Maxwell Institute for Religious Scholarship at Brigham Young University, Provo, Utah. She is the author of *Works of Love in a World of Violence*. Deidre was a research fellow at the Søren Kierkegaard Research Centre, Copenhagen, Denmark, and at the Hong Kierkegaard Library at St. Olaf College, Northfield, Minnesota. Her PhD is in women's studies from Claremont Graduate University, Claremont, California. She also holds degrees from Yale Divinity School, New Haven, Connecticut, and BYU.

I was raised in a Latter-day Saint home in which we never missed a day of family scripture reading and prayer and never missed a week of family home evening—in fact, we usually had a bonus family meeting on Sundays as well. When I was a young child, my father was the bishop of our ward. For years following his tenure, he would often muse over an incident that occurred one Sunday during Primary. Although I was unaware that my father was in the room, he observed me attempting to cajole other members of the Primary to do what I wanted them to do. He would recount that when all else failed, I indignantly puffed out my chest and with my hands on my hips, declared authoritatively to a boy about four years my senior, "I'm the bishop!" Neither my dad nor I ever seemed to remember the older boy's reaction to my ostentatious display of authority—did he cower in submission, laugh hysterically, or smirk, knowing that an overidentification with my father's role as the ecclesiastical leader of our ward gave me no license whatsoever to expect obedience from my agemates?

During my late childhood and early teen years, hearing this story retold by a bemused father, a sentimental and affectionate man who loved to tenderly reflect on various highlights of our family life, I assumed that it was humorous simply because I had falsely believed that my father's authority could—at least in moments of utter desperation—translate and extend itself into an authority of my own. However, as an adult, I came to realize that the story amused my father in a more profound way because he understood something I had not yet come to understand, namely that it was not simply my separate identity as the *daughter* of the bishop or my young age that kept me from being authorized to declare my dominant position in the Primary and expect the allegiance of other children. On a much deeper level, the scenario was laughable because I was female and therefore I was, by my very nature, precluded from ever having such authority. My audacious self-assertion was not only comical because it was so outrageous but it was also deeply ironic, nearly in a tragic sense. My words described a radically different reality from the one in which I actually existed, and they further described a reality that, at least from everyone else's perspective, never would or could exist.

Of course, this reality came crashing down on me in myriad ways during my Latter-day Saint upbringing. Constant collisions were precipitated by my belief that I could be and do anything and that I could and should think critically about and question everything, and the hypergendered world of Latter-day Saint culture in which the tacit expectation was that as a female, I would be unquestioning and con-formist about nearly everything. The incoherence went deeper: I had an intensely type A mother who structured our home life in all the typical Latter-day Saint ways, taught us to serve constantly (as just one example, we sang for and visited with the residents of a local convalescent hospital every single Sunday for most of my childhood and teenage years), and was passionately dedicated to her career and involved in other aspects of community life. Vocal about her political views as a Democrat (at least whenever my much more conservative father was out of earshot), my mom modeled for me a devotion to the restored gospel that was cou-pled with, rather than at odds with, an implacable drive for excellence and accomplishment in education and career, liberal politics, and a deep dedication to serving the wider community beyond church and family.

I remember that as a young girl, probably around the same age when I flagrantly revealed to my peers in Primary and my unsuspecting father my aspiration to ascend the rungs of the Latter-day Saint hierarchy, I sat in our chapel watching general conference with my family. Although I no longer remember the exact details of who was speaking or the particular words that were used, it stands out starkly in my memory. The general authority was describing the essential nature of women as nurturers and men as providers. It struck me that this description clashed with my lived experience—I didn't need to look past my front door in order to know that men were *not* X and that women were *not* Y. My father did more of the nurturing in our home and was only one of the providers; my mother also provided and tended to be more of a disciplinarian. Although they both worked full-time and both shared domestic chores and responsibilities, it was always clear that my dad thrived on home life while my mom flourished when immersed in work, church, and community projects.

As a teenager and young adult, I gained even more awareness about what a toll these hypergendered narratives had taken on me: I consistently internalized the messages given by Latter-day Saint leaders that women who love God and their families commit themselves to being stay-at-home mothers and that real men who love God are breadwinners who discipline their children and assert their priesthood authority within their homes. Such messages created confusion and dissonance because my basic experience of family life was that it was centered around the restored gospel of Jesus Christ, that it included innumerable expressions of love and affection, and yet did not at all reflect the rigid gender division that I was being taught was the natural outgrowth of the combination of love and discipleship.

Several years later, as a graduate student at Yale Divinity School, immersed in the study of gender and feminism in religion, I learned that from a feminist perspective, women's lived experience stood as a central authoritative source for religious, theological, and ethical reflection. Of course, in many ways this resonated loudly with my Latter-day Saint upbringing (perhaps with the exception of the qualification "women's"), which had indoctrinated within me by the time I could write my own name the belief that I could ascertain divine truth directly from its source by studying, reflecting, praying, and encountering God through resultant feelings and intellectual impressions. Much of Joseph Smith's religious project, as I understood it, was to democratize religious experience in a way that made it available to anyone who earnestly desired it enough to do the requisite work. I knew that the God who knew me intimately and would converse with me anytime I initiated dialogue between us—and often even when I didn't—had called me to pursue graduate education in religious studies and trusted me to stay faithful in the midst of the constant challenges that confronted me.

Perhaps ironically, it was these very graduate studies that could have proved subversive to my faith that illuminated for me much of the brilliance of the doctrine and theology of the restored Church of Jesus Christ that is perhaps too often overlooked and overshadowed. My studies allowed my innate belief that I could be confident in recognizing truth and could know for myself to resurface and reemerge after cultural ideas about gender had overshadowed it—in a variation of the situation of Amulek, a figure within the Book of Mormon who declared that he "knew . . . yet . . . would not know" (Alma 10:6), I found myself in the predicament of being one who knew but (in multiple ways) *could* not know, at least according to external standards. This was manifest in conversations with priesthood leaders during my early adult years, priesthood leaders who seemed to convey a confidence that they knew God's will for me better than I did, as if they could determine whether my personal conviction was right or wrong and they could hold up a trump card declaring my personal revelation to be from a diabolical source simply because it did not conform with what they took to be their revelation about me. Such experiences strained my confidence to trust myself and to know God—perhaps they also revealed why as a young girl I felt desperate to invoke a priesthood authority I did not actually have. To do so was to attempt to set a boundary between me and those who might claim to know God's will for me better than I did, an experience that often resulted in my betraying my self-understanding in order to please someone else.

Reconnecting at this time with the Christian writings of Joseph Smith's Danish contemporary Søren Kierkegaard was helpful as I wrestled with my identity as a Latter-day Saint female. For Kierkegaard, the life of faith not only condones but actually demands collision between individual behavior and universally applied expectations for the collective. In *Fear and Trembling*, Kierkegaard's pseudonym Johannes de Silentio takes Abraham's near sacrifice of Isaac as a paradigmatic example of faith because he was called privately to do something that appeared to be immoral, went against his own desires, and was seemingly at odds with God's plan. Mary, the mother of Jesus, is another important example of one who embodies such faith. Part and parcel to the life of faith is entering into a new and more intimate relationship with God that requires acting in such a way as to become inexplicable to all others—including other people who share one's same faith. What it is to live faithfully is to trust God enough to live out one's personal calling and vocation despite the criticism that inevitably comes from those who expect conformity with their own way of life. To live hopefully is to believe that God will redeem and justify such attempts at faithfulness, which generally appear as the opposite, and to live charitably is to choose not to castigate those who make judgments based on appearance rather than intent.

As a believing Latter-day Saint woman and feminist scholar who is single and childless, my life often appears unintelligible to other Latter-day Saint people, yet my path is the product of my deep and abiding faith in loving Heavenly Parents and in the Savior. Although in some superficial ways I may appear to be on the margins of The Church of Jesus Christ of Latter-day Saints, the restored gospel of Jesus Christ remains at the center of my life and of my very being; it is what centers me whenever the inevitable centrifugal forces of an often conformist culture attempt to push me out even further. The gospel calls each of us to magnify our various talents and to occupy diverse spaces in the world; the best we can do is to lift up the light of truth unapologetically in whatever mode is appropriate to each space that we occupy. Other Latter-day Saints might not accept or recognize that light for what it is when it diverges from sometimes scripted and circumscribed cultural mores, but Christ accepts and encourages our offerings nevertheless.

As a professor and mentor at Brigham Young University, I have had more experiences than I want to count of young, bright, accomplished Latter-day Saint women, many of whom are returned missionaries, confiding in me that they are "over" the Church and ready to move on to a phase of life separate from the Church after graduation. It is at times like these that I become even more grateful for parents who adapted conventional gender roles and for living a life that has never fit the mold—and for my knowing that I never could have fit the mold, even if I had tried. I am deeply grateful for the ways that Latter-day Saint culture decentered me simply because that experience motivated me all the more to seek the Savior and to establish a relationship to the divine that I might never have felt I needed or known was possible if I had the comfort of fitting in easily to Church social life. Walking alone on the water when the Savior calls can be harrowing, especially when others remain comfortably seated together in the boat; yet, it is also a space in which we come into contact with Christ in a singular way. Such a close relationship results from venturing to do the unthinkable, not from staying within the security of the status quo. This intimate and faithful way of relating with Deity proves also to be a source of authority—a source of self-knowledge and self-confidence that allows us to move forward along uncharted paths.

The Book of Mormon teaches that all those who are humble and full of faith can have "communion with the Holy Spirit" (Jarom 1:4). That is, we are able to share intimate thoughts and feelings with God. This intermingling of the divine with ourselves offers a confident footing even in the absence of solid ground. I may never be a bishop, and even if I were, I would be loath to exert the unrighteous dominion that I demonstrated when pompously threatening my fellow Primary children in a last-ditch attempt to gain their compliance with my wishes. But I no longer consider my exclamation to be either absurd or laughable—I affectionately commend my younger self for having such childlike faith in my own authority. I continually seek to engender this confidence and trust in my adult self, which requires knowing who I am as a daughter of divine Parents and who God has called me to be, as well as knowing that this divine calling transcends prescribed gender roles in an overly rigid division that would otherwise constrict and confine the expression of divine power in my life. By nature, I am not precluded from bearing divine authority, although I may limit it through my own faulty beliefs. I am decidedly *not* the bishop, but I no longer feel the need to be. I have come to know God by following divine direction and the call to an unexpected life; confidence in that relationship and trusting the experience forged as a result of it have granted me all the knowledge and authority I need.

# Letter to My Black Daughter Never Born

## ALICE FAULKNER BURCH

Alice Faulkner Burch was born in Oxnard, California, and was baptized into The Church of Jesus Christ of Latter-day Saints in 1984. She was the first African American to serve in the Chile Santiago South Mission, in which she and her companion were called as counselors in a branch presidency. She is the first Black ordinance worker in the Salt Lake Temple and serves as the Relief Society president of the Genesis Group. Alice loves doing the dying art of whole-cloth quilting and making Utah a better place for Black people to live. She is married to Robert Samuel Burch Jr.

Dearest Daughter Mine,

I know you will never read this letter but there is something within me that compels me to write it. Perhaps there will be other young women who will read it, feel a mother's love, and feel the support and encouragement they need. May it so be.

I want to talk with you, my beautiful Black Daughter, about being a Black woman in The Church of Jesus Christ of Latter-day Saints. I know what many from the African American community say: that church is evil, that church is racist, that church has a racist past. How can you be part of any organization with a racist past? How can you dishonor your ancestry and heritage like this? How can you shame your community? I have heard each of these multiple times throughout the now thirty-six years I have been a member. Sometimes it has struck my heart hard, and sometimes it has bounced off and not touched me deep, as the sayers hoped their words would.

I want to take each of these comments and talk to you about them.

THAT CHURCH IS EVIL: Remember that people say this about all churches and about all things they don't like or they disagree with. I had three mothers growing up: Mama (Elwanda Dail Faulkner), Mama's Mentor to help raise me (Bettie Patterson Bowls), and Eunice Bradford, the social worker for the state of California who took personal interest in the Black child my White Mama was raising. I loved Eunice. She did a lot for me and taught me many things. When I decided to join the Church, however, she disowned me forever, and I have never heard from her again. "That church is evil," Eunice said. "It is a racist church, and I hope they all burn in hell for how they've treated Blacks over the years." I joined anyway. I joined because God had manifested to me that it was the right path for me, that here I would find all I needed to make my way back to Him. And I believed. I still believe.

THAT CHURCH IS RACIST: The *Church* is NOT racist. There are people who are members who are racist, but the Church is not. Remember to separate the organization from the people. You will find good people and bad people everywhere you go. That includes in the Church.

THAT CHURCH HAS A RACIST PAST: Yes, it does. That is true. But if we choose not to align ourselves with every organization or company that has a racist past, there would be few places for us to attend. No Christian church is untouched by racism. Religion, as a matter of fact, is the parent of racism; a study of religion tells us that. Police departments have had racist policies; is that a reason for Black people not to become police officers in an effort to make things better? No. Some very famous and big companies today have histories of heavy racism to the point that they did not hire people of color and they made it impossible for people of color to get jobs. They hire people of color now. Is their past a reason for people of color not to work there now? No.

And, in all truth, many churches have a racist past. Incorrect interpretations of Christianity created the falsehoods of Black people being cursed, shut out from the favor of God, less-than, not equal spiritually to White people, and destined to forever be slaves. With that knowledge, if you choose not to stay or choose not to come into the Church because of that, what church is there for you to go to? I want you to know, Dearest Daughter, that regardless of its racist past and mistakes made by leaders for decades, all the ordinances you need for your life here and now as well as for your eternal salvation are contained in this Church and cannot be found anywhere else. Past is past. Truth is truth. So when you make your decision, remember that.

HOW CAN YOU BE PART OF ANY ORGANIZATION WITH

A RACIST PAST? Learn the Church's history so you understand the mistakes of the past and help people you meet not to reproduce those mistakes. Above all, remember that we each have mortal faults and failings and shortcomings. We all sin. Don't put any leader or any other person you meet—whether an apostle or the prophet himself—on a pedestal above other people, thinking they are better than, greater than, cleaner than, more pure than, or always right. Like Mama used to tell me, "There is only one perfect and completely pure person, and that was Jesus Christ. Don't look for that in anyone else." I say to you, don't look for that in anyone else. Remember, truth is truth, and all truth comes from God. Falsehood and wrong are perpetrated by people. Stay with God, my Daughter.

HOW CAN YOU DISHONOR YOUR ANCESTRY AND HERITAGE LIKE THAT? I ask, Is it dishonor to our ancestry and heritage to take upon us what is rightfully ours, what God has decreed belongs to us? Because the ordinances of life and salvation are rightfully ours, Daughter. Do not walk away from them because holding them is not an easy thing to do. The greatest blessings in life are not easy to hold. They are precious. They are more valuable than any material object you could ever possess, from large amounts of money to a famous career to a grand house to live in. Remember, truth is truth. Don't give it away too lightly or too quickly.

ALL WOMEN MUST MARRY AND THOSE WHO DON'T AREN'T AS BLESSED: The idea that all women must marry and that those who do not are not as blessed is a fallacy.[1] Another fallacy is that those who do not bear children are not as blessed. Having been single for as long as I was was hard because I listened to the fallacies people said about being single. Once I embraced being single and enjoyed it, I saw the blessings that I was given daily. I was very blessed as a single woman. Now being a married woman, I am very blessed. The truth is that God's children are all blessed. Remember, God is no respecter of persons (Acts 10:34), and He sends blessings to all who obey His commands and who seek Him.

I hope that fear of being alone will not be your motivation to marry. Marry because it is sincerely what you want to do. If you love a man, examine his character and ask yourself these three crucial questions: (1) Does he respect me? (2) What qualities does he have that I need in a husband? (3) Is our dating relationship a good enough foundation for marriage? Keep in mind that the relationship you have while dating is the relationship you have once married. It doesn't change just because you say yes.

I hope the Spirit carries the sound of my voice to you and that you feel my embrace as I speak to you, my Daughter. You belong here in this Church. It is part of your heritage to be here and to partake of the ordinances of salvation and the ordinances of exaltation. If you know truth you can navigate through falsehood because you'll recognize the difference. Seek truth. Grasp it. Hold it tight. And NEVER let it go. All your days. Now listen, I'm not saying the pathway will be easy. Goodness, no! It's going to be difficult. The way of the disciple has always been difficult.

Black people have been in this Church since its early days. Some traveled as free people with Brigham Young when he led the Saints to Utah to settle. Isaac and Jane James were one such family. Some served missions. Elijah Abel is the most mentioned of those. He served three missions. Some were bishops long before the priesthood restriction was put in place in the 1860s and removed in 1978. Joseph T. Ball was one of those. Many contributed to building the temples, like Gobo Fango, who donated $500 to build the Salt Lake Temple. Some were women, like us, who continued in faith, served our neighbors, and did our part. Amanda Chambers, Mary Ann Adams Able, and Julia Miller Lamb were three of those. Some of our sister ancestors were leaders in the larger community and today we enjoy the fruits of their labors. Alice Weaver Boozer Laggroan and Mary Lucille Perkins Bankhead were two of those. You see. Yours is a beautifully rich heritage of spiritual ancestors in this Church. And you, my beautiful Black Daughter, are the spiritual ancestor to many yet to come.

When you reflect upon me, I hope you see faith, resilience, persistence, and a true testimony. Establish a testimony born of seeking, asking, and receiving directly from God. A testimony that is kept nourished and protected with the knowledge that nothing and no one comes between your testimony and your God. The ordinances in this Church cannot be found elsewhere. All the truth you need is found through scripture study, prayer to God, and listening to His voice as He speaks to you through the Holy Spirit. The priesthood is authority directly from God. Inasmuch as any leader or any person speaks when moved upon by the Holy Spirit and speaks in alignment with the scriptures, he or she speaks the true, pure word of God. Heed the word of God and you will always be blessed. Establish a testimony of these elements because they will keep you strong during difficulties and doubts: the ordinances, the scriptures, the word of God, and the priesthood.

Dearest beloved Daughter, you will never walk alone because no one who walks with such a glorious ancestry as you have and with God is ever really alone in this world. I love you, my beautiful black Daughter. Walk always in truth, remembering that the Savior knows your name and knows your pain.[2]

## NOTES
1. 1 Corinthians 7:6–9, 25–28, 32–35; Genesis 2:18; Matthew 19:3–12.
2. See Mosiah 15:9–18.

# DAUGHTERS OF THE COVENANT

We, the children of the covenant whose eyes have been opened . . . cannot afford to live one day or one minute without being aware of the power within us.

—*Jutta B. Busche*

# My Revelation on Priesthood

## CAMILLE FRONK OLSON

Camille Fronk Olson is a professor emeritus of ancient scripture and former department chair at Brigham Young University, Provo, Utah. Her research and publications have focused on women in the Bible and Palestinian families. She loves to travel, garden, and research stories about her ancestors. She scored when she married Paul Olson, a decision that included the blessing of two children and four grandchildren.

It's funny how the same words can mean something different when we gain greater knowledge and experience in life. I have discovered this phenomenon to be true with many scripture passages, counsel from Church leaders, and especially, in my deepening understanding of the priesthood.

I grew up in northern Utah at a time when the expectations for girls pretty much began and ended with marriage, children, and home-making. My mother delighted in this role, which encouraged me to envision my life following the same path. Except it didn't.

My decision to serve a full-time mission at age twenty-one changed everything. Several people told me that guys wouldn't marry young women who served missions and that by going I would ruin my life. Saying yes to a mission also necessitated that I "take out my endowments" (the common vernacular I heard to describe one's first temple experience) when all my girlfriends were receiving the same endowment in conjunction with their temple marriages. If given a choice at the time, I would have opted to postpone going to the temple until I married. So I dreaded the day as it approached. Amazingly, those anxious feelings were swept away by the time I left the temple. I experienced a profound sense of *protection* as we traveled home. That warm feeling of safety continued the next day and again the following day when I entered the

Language Training Mission. *Protection* was the word that clearly formed in my brain when I tried to describe my temple experience. It was like I had been given an invisible covering to shield and enable me while I served the Lord. In truth, it *was* a gift from the Lord: His *endowment of power*. By the way, I still don't get the expression "taking out endowments."

I continued to rely on that enabling power after my mission. The landscape of opportunities had shifted considerably because I was a returned missionary. Doors I had never imagined opening were opening to me. I was offered a full-time position in the Church Educational System teaching seminary when no other woman at the time was similarly hired. Afterward, other open doors beckoned me, including those leading to graduate degrees and a tenure track position in ancient scripture at BYU. Meanwhile, the marriage door remained firmly shut.

This unforeseen professional life as a single woman in the Church afforded me more than two decades of grappling with many Sunday lessons and teachings about the role of women, family, and priesthood that rarely resonated with my reality. At the same time, I was immersed in daily study of scripture, ancient history, and teachings of living prophets to stay current in my field and succeed in my profession. In contrast to lessons and talks given at church, I marveled at the timelessness and power that scripture carried to reach me personally. Because scripture is not subject to change or tweaking, I had to wrestle with precise words to understand what the Lord wanted me to see. Scripture—all four standard works—more than any other form of instruction, communicated to me that even without husband or children, I was known, loved, and being guided by the Holy Spirit. I heard the voice of Jesus Christ in scripture reassuring me that I belonged and that He had a path designed just for me.

Over time, some of my perspectives for applying the gospel felt at odds with interpretations that many of my Relief Society sisters shared. Because my life experiences differed from theirs, I asked different questions and sought different opportunities to honor covenants I had made with the Lord. I found particular strength from Doctrine and Covenants 6:14: "As often as thou hast inquired, thou hast received instruction of my Spirit. If it had not been so, thou wouldst not have come to the place where thou art at this time." Days when I knew I had been directed by the Spirit, had my prayers answered, or been empowered to succeed beyond my natural abilities became my touchstone for building faith to continue down a path where few, if any, trailblazers had gone before.

In particular, I had different questions and observations about the priesthood. I don't know how many years had passed before I realized that pretty much the same questions were asked and the same comments were made every year when we discussed priesthood in Relief Society. The main question was always something like, "How does having the priesthood in your home bless your life?" Responding comments all echoed some form of gratitude for a husband who can give priesthood blessings to wife or children in time of sickness, distress, or the commencement of another school year. The gospel tenet to "sustain the priesthood" was assumed to mean support your husband and men in the Church generally to do the Lord's work.

During one lesson, my reality unexpectedly and violently crashed against these hollow-sounding platitudes. I was surprised to hear the exasperation in my voice when I asked my ward sisters, "All that I am hearing is that the main blessing of the priesthood is the convenience of a live-in blessing-giver. I live alone, but if I need a blessing, all I need to do is ask, and my home teachers will be at my door within minutes. So what am I missing because no ordained priesthood holder lives in my house?" I heard a gasp and lots of animated whispers, before a few sisters suggested the blessing of companionship or support in making decisions. So I asked, "Is that the priesthood or is that the blessing of a good marriage?"

I guess I didn't expect a satisfying answer that day because our collective foundation for discussing priesthood in Relief Society was rather thin and flimsy at the time. I could honestly argue that one could feel the Spirit in my home as readily as in a home where one or more priesthood holders dwelled. So what does "having the priesthood in your home" really mean?

My question was sincerely asked. I turned to scripture to teach me.

I remember when I discovered the verse that records the angel Moroni's words to young Joseph Smith in Palmyra, New York. Instead of citing Malachi's prophecy exactly as it reads in the Old Testament, Moroni quoted it this way: "Behold, I will *reveal* unto you the Priesthood, by the hand of *Elijah the prophet* . . ." (Joseph Smith–History 1:38; emphasis added). The verse surprised me because I expected it to read "I will ordain you to the Priesthood" or "I will give to you the Priesthood" and that it would come through Peter, James, and John or even John the Baptist. Instead, the Lord promised to *reveal* the Priesthood through the prophet Elijah.

Elijah didn't come until 1836, seven years after Peter, James, and John restored the priesthood. And he came to the newly dedicated Kirtland Temple to restore the sealing power that binds families together for generations (see Doctrine and Covenants 110:13–16). Moroni's teachings to Joseph implied that the fulness of God's priesthood would not be completely restored or its meaning completely understood by the Saints until a temple was built and the sealing power given. That necessitated the inclusion of women. This implication suggested to me that ordaining a man to the priesthood did not constitute the fulness of priesthood. I remembered the unexpected and overwhelming feelings of power and protection I had experienced after receiving my temple endowment. I knew God was the source of that power, but with what power had He endowed me?

Fast forward to the April 2014 general conference. At the time, a group of women were petitioning general Church leaders to allow priesthood ordination for women. And, for the first time, the priesthood session was publicly broadcast like all other sessions. The first speaker, President Dallin H. Oaks, issued an indirect welcome to sisters in the Church whom he must have known would be listening.[1] I was one of them. By the time he completed his discourse that evening, my eyes were overflowing with tears and my heart and mind with the Spirit. He answered so many of my questions, and he confirmed each of his teachings by citing another apostle's witness of the same truth.

Specifically, President Oaks endorsed the recent clarification by Elder M. Russell Ballard, "When men and women go to the temple, they are both endowed with the same power, which is priesthood power."[2] To clearly communicate that women are also given priesthood authority, President Oaks cited President Joseph Fielding Smith. As President of the Quorum of the Twelve Apostles, President Smith had taught nearly sixty years before, "A person may have authority given to him, or a sister to her, to do some great and wonderful things, sacred unto the Lord, and binding just as thoroughly as are the blessings that are given by the men who hold the Priesthood." Then, speaking directly to the women, President Smith declared, "You can speak with authority, because the Lord has placed authority upon you."[3] How was this teaching lost for sixty years?

As if to ensure that no one could misunderstand, President Oaks then explained, "We are not accustomed to speaking of women having the authority of the priesthood in their Church callings, but what other authority can it be?"[4] He gave examples of women receiving priesthood authority when they are set apart as full-time missionaries, officers, teachers, or any calling in the Church. My heart was doing backflips! Finally, I had the words to identify the power with which the Lord had endowed me. For decades, He has given me priesthood power and priesthood authority to act in His name as a missionary and in countless other callings. I understood why I felt insistent on being set apart before commencing a new calling. That is where my authority comes to act in His name.

Ever since that general conference, I have enthusiastically spoken of ways that women in the Church have access to the Lord's priesthood power and authority to assist in His work. I am also less patient when I hear language that confuses priesthood, "the powers of heaven" (Doctrine and Covenants 121:36), with "men who are ordained to the priesthood." As President Oaks reiterated yet again that evening, "Men are not 'the priesthood.'"[5]

Unquestionably, the word *priesthood* means far more to me today than I understood when I first went to the temple. I now feel and acknowledge priesthood power that comes from being eternally linked to ancestors and posterity. Likewise, when I hear or read about "sustain the priesthood" and "priesthood in the home," I no longer consider that those words pertain only to men in the Church. When I sustain the priesthood, I wholeheartedly confess God's unparalleled power and support given to women as well as men as they serve in His name.

The marriage door did eventually open to me, but not until I was in my late forties. I appreciate the blessing of companionship and support in making important decisions in the home. There's also a lot more laughter, goodness, and wholeness in life because of the miracle of my marriage. When I married a worthy priesthood holder, however, priesthood power didn't suddenly appear. The Lord's power was already there. My desire now is to discover the multitude of ways that the Lord is beckoning me to draw on His power to bless and assist the human family. No more bemoaning what I am not invited to do or sitting on the sidelines. Women of the Church are enlisted to fully engage on the front line. I'm all in.

## NOTES

1. Dallin H. Oaks, "The Keys and Authority of the Priesthood," *Ensign*, May 2014.
2. M. Russell Ballard, "Men and Women in the Work of the Lord," *New Era*, April 2014, as cited in Oaks, "Keys and Authority of the Priesthood."
3. Joseph Fielding Smith, "Relief Society—an Aid to the Priesthood," *Relief Society Magazine*, January 1959, 4, as cited in Oaks, "Keys and Authority of the Priesthood."
4. Oaks, "Keys and Authority of the Priesthood."
5. Oaks, "Keys and Authority of the Priesthood."

# My Wrestle with God

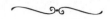

## NORMA CALABRESE SALERNO

Courtesy of the author

Norma Calabrese Salerno was born in southeastern Italy and spent part of her childhood in London. She is a graduate in Oriental studies from the Sapienza University of Rome, with emphases in Arabic and Hebrew. She is studying freedom of religion and sociocultural entanglements with globalization of religions. The mother of three girls, she loves to read and cultivate the art of slow writing while gazing from her kitchen window at the Rome Temple of The Church of Jesus Christ of Latter-day Saints, the first Latter-day Saint temple in Italy.

Dear Alessandra,

I come from having wrestled with God. I will go back to it after I have written this letter.

My dear young sister, every Sunday I see you walking sadly along the pews, reluctantly choosing a place and then helplessly sinking into your seat. I have carefully observed your melancholic disposition, and I can perceive that you feel stuck, vulnerable, and out of alignment. This liminal space you inhabit right now is blocking you, engulfing you, and pulling you away from much joy and goodness. In brief, I know you are suffering. Allow me to tell you why I believe you should be *wrestling* instead.

As a member of the restored Church of Jesus Christ in Italy all of my life, I have always had to wrestle. I was the only member of The Church of Jesus Christ of Latter-day Saints in school, in college, and in my workplace. When I was a Primary girl, my class was usually made up of only a couple of children. As a young woman, I was the only one attending Young Women on Sundays for nearly a year. Thanks to this solitary loneliness in living my faith, I have learned that it is that active and strenuous battle to know truth and establish a personal encounter with God and His Son Jesus Christ that makes us spiritually stronger, independent, and resilient during difficult times.

The wrestling I refer to involves delving, seeking, engaging, and inquiring. Our current prophet, when he was a member of the Quorum of the Twelve Apostles, said, "The Lord can only teach an inquiring mind."[1] I have always had an inquisitive disposition. Curiosity and wonder have characterized my spirit ever since I can remember. At first, however, I wasn't a patient and humble learner. As a curious teenager, I wanted to solve all the world's mysteries in a click. Furthermore, I gave credit to my mind more than my heart and eventually ended up suffocating my spirit's deep-rooted desire to grow and progress. I thought all questions could be answered by logic and reason; otherwise, knowledge couldn't be achieved. For three years I turned inside out and upside down my existential queries and doubts about the truth and sincerity within The Church of Jesus Christ of Latter-day Saints. Nonetheless, although quite skeptical, I persisted in going to church every Sunday, feeling like a suspicious investigator with a magnifying glass, sniffing out clues in every lesson, talk, and testimony I heard.

God knows us extremely well, and He knew that I could receive a testimony of the gospel only by learning to listen to my heart. I needed to open my cold, hard heart. How could He achieve that? One way was to have me gradually fall in love with the person who later became my husband, a man who managed to reply to each of my overly complicated questions with simple, faith-oriented answers. God was reaching out to me through love and other emotions that I had voluntarily chosen to repress.

As His final blow, as I literally stepped over the threshold of the chapel one Sunday, I began to cry involuntarily for no apparent reason. I didn't stop crying that day until I had totally surrendered to the Christian metamorphosis that needed to take place within my soul.[2] Armed with my shield of "human judgment and logical thinking,"[3] I had wrestled against God and the Spirit, but ultimately They had won and broken my stony, adamant heart. In return, They gave me a new one made of flesh and sinews, capable of loving others and open to revelation (Ezekiel 36:26). I had finally learned that I could access Truth "by study *and also* by faith" (Doctrine and Covenants 88:118; emphasis added). In his *Divine Comedy* Dante was basically proclaiming this same principle: There are multiple ways to reach knowledge, through visions, dreams, doctrinal dialogues, art, literature, and many other avenues. However, it is only with a "Virgil," a divine guide, what we call the gift of the Holy Ghost, that we reach the heavens, the very highest realms of Truth. That Sunday I discovered that I don't want to be "ever learning, and never able to come to the knowledge of the truth" (2 Timothy 3:7) or have a "knowledge of words, and ignorance of the Word."[4] Amid tears, I learned that science, history, and philosophy are some of the instruments to find answers and interpret reality but that "the last word does not lie with them. Every time men in their wisdom have come forth with the last word, other words have promptly followed. The last word is a testimony of the gospel that comes only by direct revelation. Our Father in heaven speaks it, and if it were in perfect agreement with the science of today, it would surely be out of line with the science of to-morrow. Let us not, therefore, seek to hold God to the learned opinions of the moment when he speaks the language of eternity."[5]

Since that momentous Sunday, I have reached out and clung to God's outstretched arm in my quest for eternal truths and have received personalized treasures and "tender mercies" in return (1 Nephi 1:2).[6]

During the following years, living in Italy has continued to shape me into a relentless wrestler. In a country where bureaucracy and not democracy reigns, with a stagnating economy and rampant corruption, I have slowly become a down-to-earth, realistic individual who is ready to unabashedly fight for my rights. Nonetheless, God always finds a way to soften my heart, which is easily prone to hardness. I like to think that God makes me do my spiritual homework every day here in Italy. For example, notwithstanding excruciatingly high rates of unemployment, it wasn't until after my fiancé and I decided to perform a truly acrobatic leap of faith that our sincerest desires to find a job were met by heavenly reward. With unwavering faith and hope, we finally resolved to set a date for our marriage, even if we had absolutely nothing on the table. After several months of fasting, praying, and searching—of wrestling—I was selected for a job, even though all the rest of the candidates were more qualified than I was.

Wrestling with God is a constant, if not an eternal, battle. Yet, it yields the sweetest and most treasured spoils of war. God wants to bless us greatly, Alessandra. We are the children of the covenant. We are of the house of Israel. It is quite fitting that one possible meaning for the Hebrew name *Israel* is "he who fights with God."[7] Wrestling matches are necessary to know Deity and receive Their revelation and blessings.[8] Brigham Young once said that "the men and women, who desire to obtain seats in the celestial kingdom, will find that they must battle every day."[9] God encourages us repeatedly to seek in order to find. It is maybe the most recurring theme and injunction found in the scriptures. With time, I have come to acknowledge that I actually *need* that wrestle, that continuous tumult of questions inside my soul, to keep me awake, alive and aglow. It is this very tension, this straining of my mental and spiritual abilities, that causes life to flow inside my every pore.

Questions are indeed opportunities for personal growth, an invitation to slow down in our fast-moving and demanding world and acquire more spiritual knowledge through patient, yet rewarding, wrestling. That is why we should never fear our questions. We should instead decide to invest in them, relying always on the help of the Spirit, for "questions can be a catalyst to real conversion if they prompt us to seek truth in the light of faith."[10] In a society of excesses, we should learn to be happy with less. Sometimes, we should thank God for what we don't have at all and even for what we've lost, because "it is when we have lost [something] that we begin to find out [its] value."[11] It is precisely that sense of loss, that yearning for eternity, which separates us from our Heavenly Parents, which triggers our questions and personal growth and ultimately sparks pure energy into our souls. Michelangelo exquisitely depicted that minimal yet profound gap in his *Creation of Adam,* which I frequently love to admire here in Rome.

I love God with all my rational mind and with all my sensitive heart. He repeatedly astonishes me with His marvelous doctrines and eccentric teachings. I love Him because He is the God who, while I was in the temple wrestling with Him to know which university course I should pursue, completely disoriented me by telling me instead whom I should marry. He continually baffles me. He stuns me. He shocks me.

In the words of my favourite hymn, I can say that I am both "amazed . . . [and] confused at the grace that so fully he proffers me."[12]

In conclusion, ours is truly an exciting dispensation of time in which to live and to wrestle. Joseph Smith, speaking to the women of the Church, the Relief Society, said, "This Society shall rejoice, and knowledge and intelligence shall flow down from this time—this is the beginning of better days."[13] Remember that those *better days* are *our* days, Alessandra. What are you going to wrestle for? Do you seek to build up or to destroy? Are you willing to do what it takes to receive God's answers? Are you patient and humble enough to accept that sometimes you might have to wait until after this mortal life to receive them? Are you ready to radically review your assumptions and pre-suppositions if God requests it?

I am not content with sound bites, of bites of the Truth. We are Italians, Alessandra, we delve into our food. We are not satisfied with a buffet; we prefer banquets. To feel truly full, we must sit down, converse with our fellow diners, and relish together the delicacies presented at the table. Fittingly, Christ's loving invitation is to come and join His feast, take a seat, and eat communally with Him, thereby experiencing a fulness of His joy.[14] His is a universal call to "every one that thirsteth" (Isaiah 55:1), that hungers, that wrestles, that struggles, whoever we are, wherever we are, regardless of our background and status.

I am "hold[ing] fast to what [I] already know and stand[ing] strong until additional knowledge comes."[15] In the meantime, I am "taking up [my] cross" (Matthew 16:24) of faith-promoting questions and follow-ing Him, passionately engaging in my own personal battles and even more fervently in His "good fight of faith" (1 Timothy 6:12).[16]

I hope and pray you are willing to do so too.

*Con amore,*

Norma

## NOTES

1. Russell M. Nelson, as cited in M. Russell Ballard, "What Came from Kirtland," Brigham Young University fireside, November 6, 1994, speeches.byu.edu.

2. See Romans 12:2; John 3:1–10; see also D. Todd Christofferson, "When Thou Art Converted," *Ensign,* May 2004; and J. Richard Clarke, "The Lord of Life," *Ensign,* May 1993.

3. Henry B. Eyring, "Continuing Revelation," *Ensign,* November 2014.

4. T. S. Eliot, *Collected Poems, 1909–1962* (New York: Harcourt Brace and Co., 1963), 147.

5. Hugh Nibley, *The World and the Prophets* (Salt Lake City: Deseret Book and FARMS, 1987), 134.

6. See also David A. Bednar, "The Tender Mercies of the Lord," *Ensign,* May 2005.

7. The etymology of the name *Israel* is the subject of much scholarly speculation. I have chosen to side with those who have its root derive from *srh,* meaning 'to wrestle.' See D. N. Freedman and Allen C. Myers, *Eerdmans Dictionary of the Bible* (Grand Rapids, MI: Eerdmans, 2000), 655.

8. Some famous scriptural "matches" are, among others, Jacob's night-long physical battle with the angel (Genesis 32:22–32), Enos's nearly twenty-four-hour wrestle before God (Enos 1:2–8), and Alma's battle with God in mighty prayer (Alma 8:10).

9. *Discourses of Brigham Young,* compiled by John A. Widtsoe (Salt Lake City: Deseret Book, 1954), 600.

10. M. Russell Ballard, "Women of Dedication, Faith, Determination, and Action,"address to Brigham Young University Women's Conference, May 1, 2015, womensconference.ce.byu.edu.

11. Arthur Schopenhauer and T. B. Saunders, *Essays of Arthur Schopenhauer: Selected and Translated by T. Bailey Saunders* (New York: A. L. Burt, 1902), 132.

12. Charles H. Gabriel, "I Stand All Amazed," *Hymns* (Salt Lake City: The Church of Jesus Christ of Latter-day Saints, 1985), no. 193.

13. Discourse given by Joseph Smith on 28 April 1842 in Nauvoo, Illinois; reported by Eliza R. Snow, in Relief Society Minute Book, March 1842–March 1844, p. 40, Church Archives, *The Joseph Smith Papers,* https://www.josephsmithpapers.org/paper-summary/nauvoo-relief -society-minute-book/37.

14. See 2 Nephi 32:3; Matthew 22; Isaiah 55:1–2; John 15:11.

15. Jeffrey R. Holland, "Lord, I Believe," *Ensign,* May 2013.

16. See also 2 Timothy 4:7.

# My Change-the-World Clock

## DIANA THOMPSON NELSON

Diana Thompson Nelson is the global advocacy director for Days for Girls International. She has a broad range of experience as an educator in the United States, China, Thailand, and South Africa. She holds a bachelor's degree in communications and a master's degree in teaching English as a second language. She loves spending time with her husband and three daughters and enjoys being active in the outdoors.

I have been a career woman since birth. When I was in elementary school, I made money selling baked goods to construction workers. When I was fourteen, I started a summer preschool business with my best friend, and I had jobs through high school. I was always looking for ways to make money. It was in my mitochondria; it contributed to my self-confidence. I liked knowing I could take care of myself, and I knew I was capable of earning a living being a professional woman. A career was for me.

I was like an apprentice clockmaker building a timepiece of my life. I knew how and when all the gears of my life should come together. I also knew if my life followed my design I would change the world. I was constructing a "change-the-world" clock. One of the gears would be an important professional career; another principal gear would be my role as a dedicated Latter-day Saint mother. I wanted both gears, and I wanted my professional gear to start immediately after college. I had it all figured out.

In the 1970s and '80s when I was growing up, Church leaders warned women about the perils of working outside the home, but that didn't worry me because in my design, working and being a mother were pieces that fit together beautifully.

After serving a mission and marrying Richard (the man of my

dreams), I focused on my studies, completing a bachelor's degree and then a master's, which put the final wind-up turns in my change-the-world clock. It was a minute after midnight, my clock was ticking in perfect rhythm, and I was ready to move forward and see where my career would take me.

And then, an unexpected alarm went off on my change-the-world clock—something I hadn't planned on. Less than one week before graduating with my master's degree, I gave birth to Lauren, the first of three daughters. When she was placed in my arms, her radiance changed my life. In an instant, to my surprise, I knew it wasn't the right time for me to work full-time. This wasn't what I had envisioned, and it was not in my grand design, which had my career gear and my mother-hood gear working at the same time. I decided to hit the snooze button for a season on my change-the-world clock and focus primarily on the motherhood gear. I didn't want to miss out on watching my daughter discover life, and I wanted to be the one to teach her those first life lessons. Consequently, I worked part-time as a university instructor in the English as a Second Language Center at Boston University. Hitting the snooze button on my career gear and focusing on this new motherhood gear was more fulfilling than I could ever have imagined.

Within a few years, after a move to a new city that brought a new part-time job at a community college, our second daughter, Maddy, came along, which accelerated my motherhood gear. After much prayer and guidance by the Spirit, I decided to quit my position at the community college and focus my full attention on raising our two little girls. A few years later we added one more girl to the family, Jenna. Our family was now complete.

With no paying job at all, I felt my change-the-world clock was now in a different time zone somewhere on the other side of the International Date Line. I honestly loved focusing full-time on my girls and volunteering opportunities, but I still had that lingering desire to be the professional woman. I often wondered why I couldn't just be content to stay at home. Why did I have this longing to do more? Despite these longings, I knew I was focused on what the Lord wanted for me, and every time I prayed, I always received the same distinct impression to "doubt not, but be believing" (Mormon 9:27). I clung to this feeling, hoping that the Lord knew my desires and that at an appropriate time in the future I would get an opportunity to realize the rest of my dream to have my own professional thing—something independent of family and church.

One day, another alarm went off on my change-the-world clock. Richard was selected to be a Foreign Service officer with the United States Agency for International Development. We were both thrilled at the opportunity this would give our family to live overseas, but I was equally thrilled at what I expected to be a new phase in which I could focus more on a career. We soon moved to Washington, D.C., the epicenter of interesting career opportunities, and I was excited. After a year of training, however, Richard was assigned to a one-year tour in Iraq without the family. That was really a tough year, and being a single mother further postponed any hopes I had of following professional pursuits. Once again, every time I prayed I felt I needed to focus on my family and to "doubt not, but be believing." I wasn't bitter, but I was really wondering if the Lord truly understood my desire to work outside the home.

Right before Richard left for Iraq, I was presented with an ironic twist that made me feel like my change-the-world clock was nearly out of batteries—our bishop called me to be the Young Women president. I was almost speechless wondering how, as a single mother, I could possibly lead the Young Women weekly activities when two of my three daughters weren't even in Young Women. On top of that, how could I manage all the meetings and other demands that come with the calling when I had no family to call upon for support? Little did I know, however, that serving in that calling was just the charge my change-the-world clock batteries needed. I loved those young women, and I learned so much from both them and the women with whom I served. Their examples and many of the conversations we had helped me to have hope that my "thing" was still there. I had to "doubt not, but be believing."

After Iraq, we all moved to Bangkok, Thailand. I thought this new opportunity might finally open doors for me professionally and that I would at last be able to realize my lifelong dream! What a surprise to learn that I was actually prohibited from working by the terms of the diplomatic treaty between the U.S. and Thailand. On top of that, I learned that I had become something known as a trailing spouse, the term used in the Foreign Service to refer to the non-Foreign Service spouse. I found the term derogatory beyond belief. I didn't need this new title to tell me I was trailing behind in my career. I was fully aware of that and felt that my change-the-world clock was ticking away precious minutes late in the day. But as always, when I would be still and pray, that same phrase, "doubt not, but be believing" would speak to my soul, and I knew, somehow, my change-the-world clock was telling the accurate time.

Then, when I least expected it, everything changed. My professional gear began to tick. Right before we moved from Thailand to South Africa, I met Celeste Mergens, the founder of Days for Girls (DfG), an international nonprofit organization focused on providing washable menstrual hygiene supplies and menstrual education to girls and women around the globe. After a few discussions with Celeste, I was hired part-time to work with their fifty thousand volunteers around the globe and to work with their independently owned and operated enterprises in southern Africa. After a year in that position, I was promoted to the role of global advocacy director. Finally, everything was coming together. My change-the-world clock is chiming loudly now as I help set up women-led enterprises throughout southern Africa and engage with governments and global organizations.

The work I'm involved in is literally changing lives. It stretches me to my limits and requires me to use my talents and gifts unlike ever before. I feel alive every day as I stress about how to move this important work forward. Clearly, the Lord knew me and my capabilities and led me to this job.

As I look back I realize three things about the path I have taken:

First, each step of the path gave me a new layer of experience that I am now drawing on to perform my work.

Second, my change-the-world clock was never actually stopped; I was just changing the world in ways I did not recognize. I see more clearly now how the Lord was using me as an instrument to change the world one lesson, one person, one volunteer activity at a time. I just didn't have a briefcase and wasn't always being paid a salary. I didn't realize until much later that my three daughters, who are all passionate global citizens, are now changing the world in their own spheres. So all those years when my focus was on them, I was laying the foundation for future change through their hands. I just didn't know it.

And, third, the Lord knew my righteous desires and fulfilled them completely; that fulfillment just played out on His timetable and in His own way, neither of which I would have been able to predict. He never forgot about my dream of having a career. I just wasn't ready for the career He knew I would be best at and which I would enjoy the most.

If I were to give my younger self some advice, I would tell her to relax, to not worry so much that her "career" was passing her by, to have faith that the Lord knew her desires, and that He was orchestrating things to work in a way that would far exceed her dreams.

# COMFORT IN CHRIST

[My] testimony has been my anchor and my stay,
my satisfaction in times of joy and gladness, my
comfort in times of sorrow and discouragement.

—*Amy Brown Lyman*

# The In Between

## JENNY REEDER

Jenny Reeder is a nineteenth-century women's history specialist in the Church History Department of The Church of Jesus Christ of Latter-day Saints in Salt Lake City, Utah. She has written two books: *The Witness of Women: Firsthand Experiences and Testimonies of the Restoration* with Janiece Johnson, and *At the Pulpit: 185 Years of Discourses by Latter-day Saint Women* with Kate Holbrook. She earned her PhD in American history at George Mason University, Fairfax, Virginia, and served a mission in the Italy Catania Mission.

Three times I've found myself in the In Between—the fragile veil between life and death. The first time I was little, and as I suffered from carbon monoxide poisoning, I floated up and watched my frantic mom pull me and my lethargic little sister out of the bathtub and rush us to the emergency room, where the nurse tugged me back down into my body. The second time happened with my first bone marrow transplant: my nurse increased the flow of my brother's stem cells into my central line, and boiling heat crawled from my chest slowly up my head. Again, I floated above, watching the events from the top corner of E-802 at LDS Hospital, until she slowed the issue of my brother's blood and pulled me back down to my leukemia-emaciated body. The third time was slow and deep: pneumonia anchored me to an oxygen tank, dragging my body for three long months along a rocky bottom until my lungs breathed clearly enough for me to untether myself and wake up for a second transplant and another chance at life.

It's like a fourth dimension, the In Between. It's a mix of past, present, and future, a reckoning of who I was with who I always saw myself becoming and who I am at this very moment. The Professional Me—a trained historian—loves digging through the past, finding crumbs left behind to recover Latter-day Saint women. Ellenor Jones was one: I love the sermon she gave to the Salt Lake Eleventh Ward Young Women in 1882. "It is well for you to remember," she wrote, "that there is no prison so dark, no pit so deep, no expanse so broad, that the Spirit of God cannot enter; and when all other privileges are denied us, we can pray, and God will hear us."[1] Ellenor knew the In Between. Born in Nashville, Tennessee, in 1832 into a mixed-race family at a time of increasing racial tension in the South, she found salvation with the Latter-day Saints in Utah, where the census counted her as white. She received her temple endowment, an unusual inheritance at the time for anyone with a drop of African blood.

It was hard to find Ellenor. She kept a low profile with no personal writings or photographs and was buried in an unmarked grave in Redding, California, in 1922. I think she wanted it that way; but now, in the safety of a changed world, she was ready to be discovered, and she called to me from the In Between.

Maybe she was with me—the Sick Me—when my blood was counted and my marrow was biopsied to find leukemia. On that fateful day, 5 November 2010, I went from being a returned missionary/marathon runner/PhD candidate/Relief Society president to being a series of medical numbers—an In Between. Every day I was weighed and measured: counting my neutrophils and platelets, my intake and output, my temperature and blood pressure. I watched as my hair fell out in clumps on my pillow and in the shower, and I remembered Alma's promise that "even a hair of the head shall not be lost" (Alma 40:23). Three baldness episodes, four recurrences, two transplants, countless chemo, radiation, and antirejection and immunosuppressant meds have crafted my runner's legs and trim frame into a four-time cancer survivor with steroid-puffy cheeks and constant viruses. Now with the marrow of two brothers coursing through my veins, I'm grateful to make it through each day, knowing that my chances of cure are slim to none. My body will never be the same—it is, after all, made from the dust of the earth (Mosiah 2:25). But I count on Abrahamic promises numbering the sands of the sea and the stars in the sky (Hebrews 11:12). And I realize, in all that multitude, that my soul—*me*—is great in the sight of God (Doctrine and Covenants 18:10). I range from the grand majesty of eternity to my smallest bit of matter.

Some people assume that God planned this to be my lot in life, sensing I would need a course correction, as if the failures of my mortal body indicate the state of my soul. Others are certain that I can be healed by living a plant-based life, or that essential oils, herbs, or coffee enemas contain the magic elixir. I, however, believe that I chose to risk mortality and with it, the chance that my imperfect DNA would slip and produce lymphocytes instead of red blood cells. I believe that my Heavenly Parents weep with me and pour blessings upon me in a variety of forms: a host of dear friends and family who fast and pray for me when my own faith wavers, capable medical professionals, the chance to wake up one more day. Someday I'll understand the abundant health promised in my patriarchal blessing or realize the Word of Wisdom promises with health in my navel and marrow in my bones (Doctrine and Covenants 89:18). Until then, I am In Between, trusting that not even one hair will be lost, even when they all fall out, because the Lord will verify His word in every particular (Alma 25:17).

After finding myself in between life and death, I've realized many ways I am In Between. I asked my oncologist if I would be able to have kids. "Jenny," he said, "you're thirty-five and you don't even have a boyfriend. You're getting older, and we don't know how your body will respond." Six years later, I'd entered premature menopause and become the Infertile Me. I am barren. Poisonous medical treatments that have saved my life have also killed my eggs. One potential life—*mine*—lost the potential of others. This predicament hurts my mother heart, piercing me to my very core. As I wander through my own dreary wilderness with noxious weeds, I expand the definition of multiply and replenish. I research and write about Latter-day Saint women's history in a magnificent career. I serve in the Church. I nurture my nieces and nephews. And here, in the In Between, I look forward to the day when I, too, will have posterity as the stars in the sky, because the Lord is not slack concerning his promises (2 Peter 1:3).

As much as I am surrounded by my host of friends and family and my women on the other side of the veil, I am verily alone. And it is not good for man or woman to be alone (Genesis 2:18; Moses 3:18; Abraham 5:14). Believe me—the Single Me—is the first one to know that. Countless priesthood blessings have promised me a faithful companion. My sweet grandad promised me that I would be married within a year. That was in 2001. The Church I was born into and that I taught about on my mission and that I continue to love reminds me so very often that the requirement of the greatest glory is marriage. And yet, I am In Between right now. I sleep on the laundry room floor during family Thanksgiving holidays because I'm the only single one. I can go to a singles ward, identified by something I'm *not*—not married. I firmly insist that I am a Latter-day Saint, that I seek holiness, and that I can fill the measure of my creation. But that's a lot of self-persuasion and discomfort. The laundry room floor is hard.

My inner-city ward for the past five years has placed me in another In Between. I am ripped out of me and made cognizant of so many other women and girls in their In Betweens. They, too, are torn apart amidst lives of addiction, abuse, disability, poverty, and ignorance. I don't understand losing children to Family Services, or being surrounded by violence, or questioning sexuality. But I do know how to rejoice and mourn and comfort, and they do too, in shockingly real ways (Mosiah 18:9). Together we muddle through, never perfectly, sometimes timely and sometimes late and always with a full heart. I make food orders, hold their hands, and call down the powers of heaven to lift them. They accept me at all stages: bald, trembling from meds, puffy from steroids. They clean my house and feed me, sometimes from their own meager supplies. But that is what we do as a Relief Society: we provide relief, and we save souls.[2] We facilitate the In Between, however we can, with whatever our spotty resources allow.

I am drawn to Mary Fielding Smith in her In Between. "It is now so long since I wrote to you," she wrote to her brother while her husband was imprisoned in Missouri, leaving her alone to care for five children. "So many important things have transpired, and so great [has] been my affliction, . . . that I know not where to begin; . . . I have, to be sure, been called to drink deep of the bitter cup." Mary goes on to describe losing her home, her possessions, and her health and arriving in a pocket of safety across the Mississippi River in Commerce, Illinois, without her husband. And just as I have, she had to learn to live with the uncertainty about what would come next. "How long we may be permitted to enjoy it I know not," she wrote, "but the Lord knows what is best for us. I feel but little concerned about where I am, if I can keep my mind staid upon God." Even in her despair, Mary finds hope, thus collapsing the past, present, and future. "I can truly say, that I would not give up the prospect of the latter-day glory for all that glitters in this world. . . . If it had not been for this hope, I should have sunk before this; but, blessed be the God and rock of my salvation, here I am, . . . having not the smallest desire to go one step backward."[3]

No way would I go backward either. I have pushed and pulled, ached and rejoiced, studied and practiced. I have crossed my own agonizing finish lines and have carried others across theirs. I don't know why I get to live while others die, but I celebrate their lives and, some day, yearn to join them. I have mourned the loss of my hair and my children in this life, but I believe in the promise of what comes after this great In Between. The ups and downs, the fronts, middles, and backs, the past and the future with the present. I believe in Christ, who mends my gaps and repairs my breaches (Isaiah 58:12).

## NOTES

1. E. G. Jones, "The Power of Prayer," in *Improvement Star* 1, no. 4, manuscript newspaper, 11th Ward Y.L.M.I.A.; reprinted in *Woman's Exponent* 10, no. 17 (February 1, 1882): 134–35; *At the Pulpit: 185 Years of Discourses of Latter-day Saint Women,* edited by Jennifer Reeder and Kate Holbrook (Salt Lake City: Church Historian's Press, 2017), 77.

2. Joseph Smith, in Nauvoo Relief Society Minute Book, 1842–1844, 9 June 1842, 63, Church History Library; *The First Fifty Years of Relief Society: Key Documents in Latter-day Saint Women's History,* edited by Jill Mulvay Derr, Carol Cornwall Madsen, Kate Holbrook, and Matthew J. Grow (Salt Lake City: Church Historian's Press, 2016), 79.

3. Mary Fielding Smith to Joseph Fielding, June 1839, in Edward W. Tullidge, *The Women of Mormondom* (New York: Tullidge and Crandall, 1877), 255–58.

# A Cup of Tea

## CELESTE A. MERGENS

Celeste Mergens is the founder and CEO of Days for Girls International. She has been featured in Oprah Winfrey's *O Magazine, Forbes, Stanford Social Innovation Review,* and was named 2017 AARP Purpose Prize Award winner, 2018 Conscious Company Global Impact Entrepreneur, and 2019 Woman of the Decade by the Women's Economic Forum. She is married to Don, her best friend, and is mother to six children and grandmother to fifteen grandchildren.

My upbringing was no cup of tea. I marvel now, however, that even the most painful experiences in my life held eventual blessings. In fact, many prepared me for my global work to help others lift themselves out of poverty, violence, and inequities. Our experience can either lift us or destroy us. For me, faith in Jesus Christ and His gospel have made the defining difference.

In a recent interview, I was asked to what I attributed my resilience. I answered without hesitation, it is my faith. I have counted on my faith to navigate the joys and challenges of day-to-day life, like air and water. Not that my faith has never been challenged. When I was a sophomore at Nathan Hale High School in Tulsa, Oklahoma, a group of students I didn't even yet know encircled me, batting the top of my head, shouting, "Where are your horns, Mormon?" That didn't deter me from expressing my belief in the Church and the blessing it had been in my life. In fact, the calm testimony I bore that day of my gratitude for The Church of Jesus Christ of Latter-day Saints gave me courage to offer them an open invitation to bat away. They quickly lost interest, and I walked on to class.

Nor was I deterred by a friend peppering me with questions about how a strong woman like me, one who stood up for women around the world, could possibly abide a church that denied women priesthood ordination, concluding with, "I can't believe my best friend is a Mormon." I didn't miss a beat in giving her my heartfelt opinion. We women can use both sides of our brain at once. We can be intuitive, judicious, and spiritual. We can be intelligent, strong, and tender. We can be the very vessels of humanity, nurturing children, our future, in the world. As a woman in this Church, I receive God's greatest power to do His work. Just not in the same way men do. To me, it's a fair balance of wondrous service.

No, the day my faith faltered was not born of those experiences or others like them when I was accosted about my religion. My moment of doubt came over a cup of tea.

A few years ago a friend, guzzling her jumbo Diet Coke filled with caffeine and deadly aspartame, asked me how I justified drinking herbal tea and hot chocolate when they were hot drinks and thus against the Word of Wisdom. I laughed and told her my choices were not harmful in any way, especially in light of the wimpy nature of my palate, which meant I don't actually manage anything hotter than lukewarm drinks. I stated with enthusiasm that I found it a miracle of prophecy that although no one knew of the danger of many substances, such as caffeine, when the Word of Wisdom was given, the Lord could still warn us to better protect our bodies without our having that knowledge. My friend and I agreed to disagree. I felt justified in what I had heard as Church counsel. I abstain from caffeine. Check.

And then came the day when caffeinated drinks seemed no longer to be a violation of the Word of Wisdom. Church headquarters and Brigham Young University suddenly began offering caffeinated beverages. In general conference, a beloved apostle confessed that a "diet soda that shall remain nameless" helped him stay awake to prepare his talk.[1] So what? Big deal. And yet . . . Suddenly, it hit me sideways. Wait. Did that mean my lukewarm hot chocolate with whipped cream on top or my lukewarm cup of mild herbal tea had been disobedient? What possible kind of sense could that make? If my understanding of the Word of Wisdom was misguided, then what else have I misunderstood? The swirl of doubt threatened me for the first time in my life. For days. Over a cup of tea.

Before you judge me a complete marshmallow (get it? chocolate and . . . ), please follow me a bit further. You see, I had considered myself someone who doesn't judge others for their choices. I know better than to judge others for what they wear to church or when they have a bad moment. But as a child I had fairly tortured one of my stepfathers over Pepsi. The poor guy would get headaches if he didn't keep up his habit, and I would say, "We are not supposed to have caffeine." Remind me to look him up to apologize after I pass from this life. I wondered how many times I had given anyone a reason to feel uncomfortable over what might have seemed a shifting principle. I wondered where else in my life I might be doing that and committed anew not to judge.

I have already received great blessings because of my obedience to the Word of Wisdom. When a health crisis hit, limiting my diet for my wellness was relatively easy because I had learned to say no to some foods and drinks. The promise to run and not be weary is real. I work with a global humanitarian effort, Days for Girls, and I usually wake before 4:30 a.m. and put in more hours than I care to admit. Not because I have to but because I have such passion and joy in what I get to be part of. I do more than I should be able to do.

I believe and have witnessed that if you are obedient, you will be blessed. Whether you misunderstood some of the details is not the point. Our willingness to be obedient is what matters. Obedience is greater than sacrifice, and the blessings are tangible. So I chose to err on the side of caution, whether it made sense or not: no more tea or hot chocolate. My interpretation would hurt no one as long as I didn't hold others to it. At the very least I was sincerely showing my own commitment to the Lord.

But my heart had one response: "Are you kidding me right now?!" I wanted to understand. I turned back to the actual commandment in the scriptures. The Word of Wisdom was "given for a principle with promise" (Doctrine and Covenants 89:3). A principle is an enduring truth, a law, a rule you can adopt to guide you in making decisions. Generally principles are not spelled out in detail. Leaders teach us the principle together with the promised blessings. We then figure out how to apply it to ourselves.

As I pondered, I realized we get caught up in a lot of Sunday dinner roasts. Do you know the story of the woman who was preparing a roast for Sunday dinner when her mother asked why she cut off the ends? The daughter said, "That's how you always prepared it." The mother replied, "That was only because our oven was too small for a proper roast pan."

Sometimes we get caught up in our personal focus on facets of Church culture and forget to go back to the source to study for ourselves and prayerfully seek for how a principle applies to our own life, all the while checking ourselves not to judge others. Small things can trip us up in a big way.

Here's my witness. Success in navigating the Lord's admonition is about the principle, the promise, and a prayerful search for how it applies to us very personally. In the process, it's easy to skip over key points. As I studied, the principle became clearer, and I went from concern to a chuckle. Good grief. I had made caffeine a commandment in my life, and it says right in the scriptures, "Not by commandment or constraint, but by revelation and the word of wisdom" (Doctrine and Covenants 89:2). Reading on, I was reminded, "And all saints who remember to keep and do these sayings, walking in obedience to the commandments, shall receive health in their navel and marrow to their bones; and shall find wisdom and great treasures of knowledge, even hidden treasures; and shall run and not be weary, and shall walk and not faint" (Doctrine and Covenants 89:18–20).

I have seen these blessings. I count on them. I can be obedient, even stalwart, and never need to judge anyone else for their own interpretation. The journey to understanding many things is ongoing and filled with the sweetness of asking and receiving a personal answer of assurance. That's amazing to me. Still learning. Check.

NOTE
1. Dieter F. Uchtdorf, "O How Great the Plan of Our God!" *Ensign,* November 2016.

# Receiving the Temple

## WENDY ULRICH

Wendy Ulrich, PhD, MBA, is a psychologist, former president of the Association of Mormon Counselors and Psychotherapists (AMCAP), a consultant with the RBL Group, and founder of Sixteen Stones Center for Growth in Alpine, Utah. Her books include *Let God Love You: Why We Don't; How We Can; The Temple Experience: Passage to Healing and Holiness; Live Up to Our Privileges: Women, Power, and Priesthood;* and the *Wall Street Journal* best seller, *The Why of Work: How Great Leaders Build Abundant Organizations That Win.*

Macy Robinson

There are Sundays when I don't get a lot out of attending church. My ministering efforts often leave me feeling inadequate at love, I'm not crazy about the welfare farm, and I have to push my introverted self to attend ward activities. I would probably benefit from figuring out how to do such activities differently, but I'm glad I am still welcome at them even if I participate more generously and joyfully in other ways. I still have something to give and much to receive.

I've also had long periods when I didn't get much from the temple. Likewise, I've had breakthroughs when I learned and felt things of great value there. I seem to receive the most when I go more often, go with others as well as alone, participate in a variety of ordinances, and *feel* as well as think my way through them. I sometimes think of the temple as a spiritual gym—a place to practice spiritual skills, receive coaching and support, get old injuries addressed, and gain strengths that will help me outside its walls—rather than as a history or sociology class, or a church meeting, or a service project.

And what is it I'm practicing in this spiritual gym? Finding God. Specifically, finding God while traveling through a lonely, confusing, demanding world that regularly reminds me of my spiritual weaknesses—impatience, judgmental attitudes, fear, shame, ignorance, irritability, distraction, boredom, laziness, and susceptibility to temptation, among others—all things I work on in that spiritual gym, often straining with the effort.

My first experience in the temple was receiving my endowment. My father had gone to the temple once and never returned, and because I did not want to replicate his experience, I had asked lots of questions, studied, fasted, and prayed in preparation for a life-changing, spiritually empowering experience. I came away a little taken aback and needing some time to process. Even so, there were moments that touched me deeply, taking me into a world removed and set apart from the ordinary, and I left that world feeling for the first time in my twenty-one years like an adult woman instead of a girl.

Over the next decade or so I jumped into a mission, then marriage, then parenting in rapid succession, living mostly in places where the nearest temple was hours away. I continued to go from time to time, and sometimes I had a sweet experience or a meaningful insight, but I was also frustrated that I wasn't understanding more. I was at least reassured that I was not alone when I read President David O. McKay's observation:

"I have met so many young people who have been disappointed after they have gone through the House of the Lord. They have been honest in that disappointment. Some of them have shed tears as they have opened their hearts and expressed heart-felt sorrow that they did not see and hear and feel what they had hoped to see and hear and feel."[1]

Eventually I decided it was time to put more spiritual and intellectual effort into the temple, prompted in some measure by a miraculous experience with family history that convinced me one of my deceased ancestors *really* wanted her temple work completed. I decided if she cared about those ordinances that much, maybe I needed to figure out why. I began to pray and study and ponder more earnestly. And, distilling like dews from heaven (Doctrine and Covenants 121:45), ideas, feelings, and changes gradually came. It has helped for me to do the following:

*Spend concentrated time.* I live ten minutes from a temple now and I go almost every week, but I learned so much during a time when the closest temple was five hours away that I periodically try to replicate the experience of attending an endowment session alone or with loved ones, quietly sharing impressions or questions afterward, and then repeating that experience again and again. Each of these rhythms has advantages, but I have learned that I actually become more attentive, not less, when I go more frequently or do several ordinances in a day.

In my training as a psychologist, I learned to think of every part of a dream as a part of me. (How am I like this parachutist, or baby, or guerilla in my dream? What part of me is represented by this red ticket, or my mother, or the ocean? How is my life like this bike ride, or dance, or room?) I have noticed that the temple is more like a dream than a history, and I learn a lot by thinking of every part of the temple—every person represented, every name, every gesture, every piece of clothing, every symbol portrayed—as a part of me. I note that Christ often compares Himself in scriptures to a female (3 Nephi 10:4–5; Numbers 19:1–9; Isaiah 49:15–16), and I have needed all my life to liken myself to stories of men in the scriptures (1 Nephi 19:23). So it makes sense that women and men can both compare themselves to each person portrayed in the temple without assuming that women should learn only from women or that men should learn only from men. "All are alike unto God" (2 Nephi 26:33).

*Check my sexist assumptions at the door.* We have become more sensitive in recent years to society's differing assumptions about how men and women are to be treated and valued, and we try to change sexist assumptions that are unfair or limiting to either sex. I've noticed, however, that sometimes I have assumed a word or action is denigrating or unfair to women even when there are other legitimate possibilities. For example, in a worldly marriage ceremony, I often think it rather sweet for a father to give the bride away, but it took me a long time to even notice who used to give the bride away in the temple. I don't think it is condescending to call God our *help* (Psalm 46:1; Exodus 18:4), or insulting to an important male figure in the temple drama to be *silent,* or denigrating to the priesthood to say it is *given* to someone. Yet I have sometimes brought different assumptions and associations to such terms when applied to women. Sometimes I have also failed to notice the priestly roles performed by women in the temple.

Temple language is changed periodically to more accurately communicate to diverse or changing cultural sensibilities. Meanwhile, when sexist assumptions or expectations sneak into my temple experience, remembering my conviction that God is completely fair, loving, and good has helped me search out more benevolent explanations instead of clinging to more limiting ones.

*Remember I'm there to be empowered and to empower others.* When I was set apart as a temple worker, I was authorized to use the priesthood in the temple to bless the temple patrons and charged to do so with priesthood power. Only gradually did I realize that priesthood authority and power were conveyed to me from the time I first received my endowment and that upon every return to the temple I was helping to convey that authority and power to others. Now I am particularly invested in learning how that power can apply outside the temple in all my interactions and in my personal relationship with God. That I am not given priesthood ordination or office does not mean I am not given priesthood authority or power. The temple tutors me in why and how.

*Assume it will take time and practice.* Yes, some things in the temple still confuse me. But I'm grateful for these observations by C. S. Lewis:

"If our religion is something objective, then we must never avert our eyes from those elements in it which seem puzzling or repellant; for it will be precisely the puzzling or the repellant which conceals what we do not yet know and need to know."[2]

"Science progresses because scientists, instead of running away from such troublesome phenomena or hushing them up, are constantly seeking them out. In the same way, there will be progress in Christian knowledge only as long as we accept the challenge of the difficult or repellant doctrines. A 'liberal' Christianity which considers itself free to alter the faith whenever the faith looks perplexing or repellent must be completely stagnant. Progress is made only into a resisting material."[3]

I've had the opportunity over several decades to push against things I have not understood before some have eventually shifted, either in the temple or in me. I'm grateful for ongoing revelation that allows modifications in the temple and the Church to more accurately communicate the gospel to expanding cultures and contexts (even though I'm surprised to find I sometimes miss old forms, even ones that once concerned me). But I'm also grateful for the patience and persistence I've learned from wrestling with the Lord over things I have not understood, even when eventually they were altered. It is not by accident that God's covenant people are called the house of Israel, named after Jacob, or Israel, who wrestled with God until, in some mysterious way, they each prevailed (Genesis 35:10; see footnote *a*).

I have learned, and am learning, to truly rejoice in the temple, "the house of the daughters of Zion" (Doctrine and Covenants 124:11), the "house of *my* pilgrimage" (Psalm 119:54; emphasis added), the holy place where the Spirit is teaching me holiness, including by letting me struggle. God is building not just hundreds of temples in our day but millions, and we are those temples (1 Corinthians 6:19; Doctrine and Covenants 93:35). I rejoice, indeed I am awed, to realize I can acquire the power of my Heavenly Parents in time and in eternity and that I can in turn share that power with all the generations to follow.

## NOTES

1. David O. McKay, "Temple Address," September 25, 1941, http://emp.byui.edu/satterfieldb/pdf/DavidOMcKay'sTempleSermon.pdf.
2. C. S. Lewis, *The Weight of Glory* (New York: HarperCollins, 1949), 34.
3. C. S. Lewis, "Christian Apologetics," 1945, https://virtueonline.org/christian-apologetics-cs-lewis-1945.

# Hoping for Joy

## HOLLIE RHEES FLUHMAN

Hollie Rhees Fluhman graduated from Brigham Young University, Provo, Utah, with a BS in family science, which has proven to be mostly useless during the past twenty-two years of raising her family. Indeed, she now regards family life as emphatically unscientific. She has enrolled again at BYU in post-baccalaureate studies and wrestles with Latter-day Saint women's history and academic women's studies. She lives in Provo with her family and is most fortunate to be married to Spencer, her favorite person in the world.

We found ourselves at a beach house we were inclined to covet. Nine-year-old Sadie and I wandered through the morning marine layer alone and wondered at the deafening silence of crashing waves. The sea air, gritty with salt and sand, polished my soul's sharp edges more than most therapists could. Gradually, peace replaced chaos in this mother's soul, if only for a morning. For her part, Sadie squealed with delight as she ran toward the water. She spotted a pod of dolphins and raced back and forth, singing and arms flailing, in some kind of communion with the animals.

But moments pass. Sunburns and a little sand in our eyes marked a benediction on that glorious morning. On those covetous, beach-house mornings, it was tempting to believe that coastal living is a prescription for lasting joy. My disciple-self knows that it is not, any more than are fame, fortune, or physical perfection.

But I have learned the hard way that the typical gospel answers we give to the question "What brings joy?" are often oversimplified. Somewhere during my gospel upbringing, I adopted the delusion that doing everything right (scripture reading, daily prayers, temple attendance, family home evening, and so on) would lead uncomplicatedly to endless joy. In my adolescent mind, joy meant a happy family (i.e., no one has problems) and a comfortable life (i.e., no worries about money).

Certainly a beach house would have fit nicely within that vision. Joy in my young mind equated, essentially, to the absence of real-world problems. It wasn't about becoming anything or growth or service; it was a fictive world where righteousness spares us trouble of any kind. Where did this delusion come from? Is it a misinterpretation of the prosperity verses in the Book of Mormon? Was it overly rosy church lessons? Was I missing some balancing messages along the way? Regardless of where the fault lies, I've found that many of us find sooner rather than later that joy isn't mechanical or simplistically formulaic. Sometimes folks who make really bad choices have the beach houses and sometimes the consecrated languish in the fiery furnace. Most of us fall somewhere in between.

I *did* graduate from college, I *did* marry my dream guy in the temple, and I *did* have four brilliant children. We *do* read the scriptures, serve in the Church, have family home evening, and attend the temple fairly regularly . . . and every day is *very* hard work. My adolescent dream scenario has turned out like our beach day. The transcendent moments of peace often seem fleeting and too rare amidst the proverbial sunburns and sand in our eyes.

And so I have had to rethink joy. Adam Miller's poignant paraphrase of Romans 9 reads, "Certainly it's true that so many of life's favors and troubles have nothing to do with what we've earned or deserved. They come and go, indifferent to us, with a logic all their own."[1] If that's the case, and my experience tells me it is, no amount of consecrated gospel living can *assure* endless days of bliss. With a "spiritual reward" system so mysterious, how in the world am I to find joy in this life? Can joy thrive in a world of both startling beauty and unpredictable, even undeserved, pain?

I have found that the most profound sources of joy can also generate profound pain. Motherhood has certainly taught me that. My sweet mother has a saying that has proven to be painfully true for me. When considering the struggles of my children, she has said, "A mother is only as happy as her saddest child." (This is to say nothing of the pain of women who want marriage or motherhood and don't have them.) One of the unintended consequences of all our emphasis on nurturing and mothering, which in itself is unquestionably good, is that we women often take responsibility for the happiness of everyone around us. This adds a double burden—not only do we ache with our children in their pain but we also tend to see their struggles as somehow failures in ourselves. For women like me, President David O. McKay's oft-recited (still, after eighty-four years) counsel, "No other success can compensate for failure in the home," can feel like a perpetual indictment.[2] I have long felt that failure of any kind in our home was on me—my responsibility, my fault. It seems like a fool's errand to pin my joy on others. But these habits of mind and heart are hard to break. Pain and suffering aren't necessarily synonymous with failure, I know, but logic rarely trumps emotion for this mother.

Latter-day women have been wrestling with the problems of joy and pain since the beginning of the Restoration. In 1986, a brilliant Church leader named Francine Bennion gave a talk at the BYU Women's Conference called "The Theology of Suffering." She would have unraveled my adolescent delusion had I heard her then: "I think suffering on this earth is an indication of God's trust, God's love. I think it is an indication that God does not want us to be simply obedient children playing forever under his hand, but wants us able to become more like himself. In order to do that we have to know reality. . . . If we are to be like God, we cannot live forever in fear that we may meet something that will scare us or that will hurt us. We have to be able, as he is able, to meet what comes of others' agency."[3] I have discovered that such suffering can create fertile ground for humility, which in turn might be the critical environment for real seeds of joy to grow. Without humility, we find ourselves casting about wondering why the world has done us wrong. Every one of us knows someone who has no business being as happy as they are. Inevitably, they are humble. I don't mean the false-modest acknowledgment of a weakness or two. I mean the kind of humility that often grows from the cracks of brokenness. It is the kind of broken-heartedness that recognizes that without the Savior's healing love, we are nothing. Joy is made manifest against the bleak backdrop of the pain and suffering that seem inescapable in this life.

My spirit at times has been nearly smothered by depression.

Sometimes, the darkness is thick enough that spiritual light is difficult even to perceive. My life is generally good, yet the darkness can linger senselessly and interminably. Genetics, brain chemistry, and hormones are a tricky business and often leave me in a general fog but especially numb to spiritual things. Ironically, when I am most desperate for His light, I seem most blind to it. In those stretches, reading, praying, and attending the temple often give little comfort even though I continue to do them in faith. If I can't feel God's love, how do I trust that He is real? For me, that is when it becomes necessary to heed Elder Dieter F. Uchtdorf's inspired counsel, "Doubt your doubts before you doubt your faith."[4] So I sift through and cling to past spiritual experiences—to memories—wringing from them the strength to push through to the light I hope will come.

A friend reminded me that the Jaredites' vessels would be "buried in the depths of the sea, because of the mountain waves which broke upon them, and also the great and terrible tempests which were caused by the fierceness of the wind" (Ether 6:6). The tempest, though fierce, was the force carrying them to the promised land. Are our tempests taking us to the place God wants us to be? Does trusting Him require that we are sometimes "buried in the depths"? Is He still with us in the depths? In the darkness?

His answer to the Prophet Joseph Smith's prayer in the Liberty Jail shouts that He is: "If the heavens gather blackness, and all the elements combine to hedge up the way; and above all, if the very jaws of hell shall gape open the mouth wide after thee, know thou, my son, that all these things shall give thee experience, and shall be for thy good. The Son of Man hath descended below them all. Art thou greater than he? Therefore, hold on thy way. . . . Thy days are known, and thy years shall not be numbered less . . . for God shall be with you forever and ever" (Doctrine and Covenants 122:7–9).

Believing that means I must acknowledge His presence with me both on beach mornings and in the devastation of depression.

Here at midlife, I see clearly that joy is not what remains when troubles end. Instead, joy is a way of wending our way through the peaks and valleys of life. Our Church rhetoric about broken hearts and feeble knees sometimes seems like understatement. If language can fail to express the pain we carry in the body of Christ, the same probably holds true for the joy that can find us along the way. The joy I feel in my life has not come because my life has been easy or glamorous. (Though sometimes it is easy and on rare occasion it has flirted with glamorous.) Joy seems both elusive and persistent in my gospel living. Sometimes, it is apparent only in retrospect. Sometimes, I'm jarred into recognition of it by some unexpected event or fellow-traveler. For me, joy has come up through the cracks, when brokenness has given way to some new insight or some new way to love. It's not easy to continue on the road of discipleship with such a fraught faith. But time and again God gives me reasons to keep believing, keep loving, and keep reaching out beyond myself. So, I will get out of bed tomorrow and hope for joy.

## NOTES

1. Adam S. Miller, *Grace Is Not God's Backup Plan: An Urgent Paraphrase of Paul's Letter to the Romans* (self-published, 2015), 48.

2. J. E. McCulloch, *Home: The Savior of Civilization* (Washington, DC: Southern Cooperative League, 1924), 42, as cited in David O. McKay, in Conference Report, April 1935, 116.

3. Francine R. Bennion, "A Latter-Day Saint Theology of Suffering," in *At the Pulpit: 185 Years of Discourses of Latter-day Saint Women,* edited by Jennifer Reeder and Kate Holbrook (Salt Lake City: Church Historian's Press, 2017), 229.

4. Dieter F. Uchtdorf, "Come, Join with Us," *Ensign,* November 2013.

# ACKNOWLEDGMENTS

We gratefully acknowledge the women who inspired this collection—daughters, mothers, students, and friends. The authors' stories proved true our hunch that Latter-day Saint women's voices could continue to inspire the whole of the body of Christ. We thank the Neal A. Maxwell Institute for Religious Scholarship at Brigham Young University for material and moral support. Melissa DeLeon Mason provided critical collaborative vision early on. We express gratitude to Lisa Roper and Laurel Christensen Day at Deseret Book Company for their support and encouragement. We likewise thank readers and peer reviewers who strengthened the manuscript. Our immediate and extended families first applauded the idea of this book and cheered us on at every step—to them we express our deepest love.

—Hollie Rhees Fluhman and Camille Fronk Olson

# PART SOURCES

The quotations on the part pages are from the *Ensign, Daughters in My Kingdom: The History and Work of Relief Society* (2011, 2017), or *At the Pulpit: 185 Years of Discourses of Latter-day Saint Women* (2017). Specific references can be found in the following locations:

## DOING TRUTH
Elaine A. Cannon, "Season of Awakening," *At the Pulpit*, 210.

## DIVINE IDENTITY
Sheri L. Dew, "Knowing Who You Are and Who You Have Always Been," *At the Pulpit*, 267.

## UNITY IN SISTERHOOD
Elaine L. Jack, *Daughters in My Kingdom*, 94.

## DIVINITY IN MOTHERHOOD
Julie B. Beck, "A 'Mother Heart,'" *Ensign*, May 2004.

## CAREER AND FAMILY
Mattie Horne Tingey, "The School of Experience," *At the Pulpit*, 86.

## TRIUMPH OVER TRIALS
Francine R. Bennion, "A Latter-day Saint Theology of Suffering," *At the Pulpit*, 217.

## CONTINUED EDUCATION
Bathsheba W. Smith, "We Have Still a Greater Mission," *At the Pulpit*, 100.

## LEARNING BY STUDY AND ALSO BY FAITH
Elsie Talmage Brandley, "The Religious Crisis of Today," *At the Pulpit*, 139.

## DAUGHTERS OF THE COVENANT
Jutta Baum Busche, "The Unknown Treasure," *At the Pulpit*, 239.

## COMFORT IN CHRIST
Amy Brown Lyman, *Daughters in My Kingdom*, 79.